Homeschool
HIGH SCHOOL
Made Easy

Find Your WHY . . . then Find Your WAY

By Lea Ann Garfias

ISBN: 9781521903155

First Edition: July 2017

10 9 8 7 6 5 4 3 2 1

To Gian, the world's most successful guinea pig.

You did it!

And to Adana, who makes homeschooling

high school look good!

Table of Contents

Introduction

When you homeschool YOUR way – even homeschooling high school – everything is simple.

HIGH SCHOOL DOES SEEM a lot more challenging than the earlier years of homeschooling. I have to be honest, when my husband mentioned to me that it was time for our oldest to start high school, I burst into ugly crying. In the middle of the grocery store. I could not stop sobbing about it for a couple of days. I am a homeschool graduate and had been homeschooling over a decade, but I still felt completely overwhelmed by the enormity of the responsibility. *I am supposed to completely prepare this young person for adulthood? I can barely adult myself!*

7

Now that student has graduated, and I now confidently homeschool two more teens (and their younger siblings are right behind them). Do you know what I've learned? The high school years really are so much simpler than I thought. The deeper we get into high school, the clearer the path becomes.

Yes, I have changed a few things in my homeschooling since graduating our first student. My perspective on homeschooling has definitely matured over the years, and the important priorities have crystallized. There are many things I wish I had understood right from the beginning, ideas and strategies that would have made our days much smoother and my sleep much easier. I want to share those with you.

What is this book about?

I'm so glad you asked! While I briefly covered high school in my previous book, *Homeschool Made Easy*, I found my readers wanted even more. Since that book, my list of topics has just multiplied. I asked my friends on Facebook, my homeschool mom buddies, and my blog readers for more burning questions and found even more questions to answer:

- Why is homeschooling the right choice for high school?
- How does a mom know if she *can* homeschool high school?
- What do high school students need to know?
- Should we or should we not take outside classes?
- What about these hard subjects?
- What unique social challenges do high school students face?
- How do family dynamics change in high school years?
- How do homeschool families navigate teen issues like dating, driving, working, and parties?
- Should we prepare our students for college or for a vocation?
- How do we handle transcripts, tests, entrance essays, and scholarship applications?
- How do we know if the student is ready for *real life*?

In my previous *Homeschool Made Easy,* I gave an overview to homeschooling – how to make the decision, how to make it easier, and what to do each stage from preschool through elementary and middle school and even high school. My goal was to simplify the homeschool process for you right away so that no matter what educational stage your student is in, you can recapture your purpose in your homeschool and rekindle your student's love of learning.

This book goes a step further.

Actually, we will dive furloughs deeper into high school. I will help you sweep aside all the distractions and frustrations and fears that threaten to derail your attempts to finish homeschooling. Then you can reconnect to your overriding purpose to *make sure homeschooling is a success for your family*. Finally, we will use that newfound purpose to reframe all the other questions and issues you face in the high school years.

By the end of this book, you will find that **your *why* really does direct the *way* you complete high school**.

I am so excited you are homeschooling high school. As a homeschool graduate, mother of a homeschool grad, and an in-the-trenches homeschool mom myself, I lift my coffee mug to you in solidarity. You can do this. And I'm here to help. Seriously. Got questions? Send me a message anytime at leaann@lagarfias.com.

Your friend,

Lea Ann

(who has traded in the ugly-crying for drinking coffee, rolling on essential oils, and laughing with my teens)

1. Why Homeschool High School?

*Love the Lord your God with all your heart and with all
your soul and with all your strength and with all your
mind, and love your neighbor as yourself.*
(Luke 10:27)

MOST HOMESCHOOLERS start off in the beginning for just "one year at a time" during the elementary years, trying out the homeschool lifestyle to see if it works for their family culture. I put that "one year at a time" in quotes because this has become an infamous homeschool phrase. We all get sucked in to try it for "just one year," and then we are hooked. Even me.

I did *not* initially want to homeschool, but my husband told me to try homeschooling our preschooler for "just one year," and that is the end of the story.

Maybe you started homeschooling to overcome learning difficulties, to help your gifted child reach his full potential, or to better meet the challenges of your special needs student. Perhaps you wanted to avoid bullying, negative peer pressure, and other worldly influences in the public school system. You may have even set out to give your child a firm moral foundation, to pass on your own values and principles, to prepare the young person for a lifetime of worship and ministry.

Then high school comes along, and you are tempted to quit.

The teen years are too difficult, the high school subjects too demanding, the social pressures and hectic schedules and graduation requirements too scary. Parents who begin with all the best intentions find themselves unable, unwilling, and unprepared to meet the demands of high school. So they put the student back into public school.

I nearly did the same thing.

The teen years are already super hard on parents. You've got hormones, you've got relationship issues, you've got identity struggles, you've got separation difficulties . . . and your teen does, too (ha!). This makes for rough going for a few years. There are also the academic and parenting pressures of launching a new adult into the world. It seems way easier to just pack up the teacher's manuals and put everyone back on a bus.

But maybe we have it all wrong.

What if instead of freaking out (like I did), instead of giving up (like I wanted to do), instead of stressing out about homeschooling high school (like maybe I occasionally still do) . . . what if instead, we reinvent the entire process? What if we simplify everything, strip homeschooling to the foundation, and find our purpose, our calling, our joy – and then pass this on to our young people?

Find the Purpose in YOUR Homeschooling

It's time to recommit yourself to *why* you are homeschooling your teens. For these high school years, connecting to your values remains more important than ever. Your homeschool *why* – that purpose, that commitment – will change everything. Your homeschool *why* refocuses your teaching, defines your curriculum, guides your choices, and ultimately simplifies your high school journey.

For my own family, there are four main reasons my husband and I continue to homeschool during the high school years. These goals shape our education, our activities, our entire family life. Maybe you will identify with some of these homeschool values. Perhaps you will add more priorities for your own family.

1. To pass on our values to our teens

The teen years become a most critical time to reinforce beliefs, principles, and values that shape the rest of life's decisions. Now's not the time to give up, but rather to dig in.

Teens are hypersensitive to inconsistency and (dare we say it?) hypocrisy. They yearn to experience a life of meaning, and they want to see actions lining up with lifestyle. They've been promised all through childhood that God is good and that clean living pays (so to speak), and they are looking for evidence that the

16

world runs consistently with the principles we have been teaching them.

They want to see us live our faith.

Mom, the single most valuable lesson you will ever teach your children is to love God and love others. These teen years represent our greatest opportunity to walk the walk, to humble ourselves before our children, to transparently share our spiritual journey, and to help them launch out on their own.

If we can keep this perspective, if we can stay laser-focused on that ultimate goal, the rest of our fears and frustrations will fall away. When we seek God's best for our teens while humbly admitting our own inadequacies, we will find the Spirit's supernatural enabling for each day.

2. To teach academics with a purpose instead of pressure.

Hey, I know academic pressure. As a teen back in the early years of the homeschool movement, I remember the stress of proving to homeschool was legitimate, when my parents saved every test and

17

worksheet, every percentage point was scrutinized, every college entrance exam becoming a measurement of worth. Now a homeschool parent, I am keenly aware that every *A* seems to be worth thousands of dollars in college scholarships, every *C* feels like a personal failure, every essay and test measuring whether we should or should not be trusted with the education of our own offspring.

Yet, I do not want to teach to the test. I do not want to measure my student's success on a number scale. I do not want to tie test-taking or communication skills with financial incentives. The broken educational institutions around us fail young people that way. Homeschooling should be different.

Nevertheless, it takes faith to spend more time understanding than regurgitating. It takes faith to wrestle with the messy truths of history rather than memorizing pithy sayings. It takes faith to slow down math to learn the principles instead of the shortcut.

When we connect with *why* we are homeschooling, when we remain true to our convictions about who God created our young people to be and the kind of difference He desires in their lives, then the distractions of grades and tests and arbitrary standards grow dim. We find a new focus on the purpose of each day's lessons, and we find a new vision for a lifetime of learning.

3. To guide our teens through relationships.

One of the most significant changes in the teen years is in how they view relationships with friends and with the opposite gender. Young people desire close friends and learn painful lessons about cliques, gossip, and breakups. They notice boys and girls in a new way and closely watch their friends flirt, date, and break up. They experience powerful temptations. They define what kind of friend, what kind of boyfriend or girlfriend, and even what kind of spouse they will become.

This is all super hard.

Some people homeschool to try to avoid all those messy teen dramas. Others send their teens to school thinking teens need to be around more of all that socialization. In reality, homeschooling allows us to

19

walk alongside our young people through these experiences, offering comfort, counsel, and protection as they make life-long connections to people from a variety of backgrounds, experiences, ages, and even beliefs.

Diversity represents a painful struggle in our culture. Homeschool teens have a distinct opportunity to represent biblical love, sensitivity, and unity within their communities and churches. We as parents must demonstrate the courage and humility to reach out first, ourselves. Our relationships within our family and without the community teach powerful lessons to our teens.

4. To prepare our teens for responsible, productive adulthood.

Through the teen years, we take definitive steps to train our teens for adult life. They work jobs out of the home. They pay bills. They manage their time and their finances. They participate in ministries and community events. They choose a college and figure out how to pay for it. They take responsibility for their

20

own mistakes and learn how to live with consequences. We have said many times that if our teens can survive high school with us as well as their first couple of years at college on their own, we will never worry about their adult lives. They will have the tools and experience they need to keep going.

Isn't that what homeschooling – and all of parenting – is about: showing our young people how to have a relationship with God, teaching them to love others, preparing them to fulfill their responsibilities to God and man?

These are our family's four most significant principles for homeschooling high school, goals that define what we are doing and why. You might notice what we left off of our list: college acceptance, giftedness training, career launching, isolation from the outside world, controlling their choices. Those motivations may be central to some homeschoolers, but they are completely peripheral to the Garfias family homeschool *why*.

When we keep our priorities in focus, all of the rest is simplified. Don't believe me? Turn the page for how you can make homeschooling high school easy.

2. Preparing for High School

Well begun is half done.

-- Aristotle

WITH TEENS, WELL PREPARED in middle school is half the battle of high school. If teens already know what to expect, how to study, and where to focus, they will begin high school with confidence . . . maybe even enjoyment (I said maybe). There are several things middle school students and parents can do to ease the high school transition, helping smooth the way for a successful freshman year.

In fact, preparing preteens for high school work is one of the primary purposes of middle school. Students cannot successfully jump from elementary-level work to high school; a lot of mental and academic maturing needs to occur first.

Remember, the elementary years concentrated on the basics of education: how to read, how to write, how to use numbers to express truths, how to memorize facts. Your student concentrated on the *basics* of learning.

Now in the middle school years, students begin looking for connections to a bigger picture: how to read and research for deeper understanding, how to write paragraphs and papers to express their thoughts, how to express unknown ideas and complicated processes with numbers and words. They are moving from the knowledge stage to the understanding stage, from grammar to dialectic.

During this brief time, our students go through great changes. Their bodies rapidly grow and change through puberty. Their emotions deepen and explode. Their minds develop rapidly, challenging what they know and longing to understand what they don't. This is when young teens develop the healthy habits, character qualities, and study skills that will ensure high school success.

What if it seems too late, your student is already in high school? Don't despair! There is always time to catch up! Study this list of goals and find areas your student can improve, then take steps now to train these habits. Instead of taking a year or two to practice, you can concentrate for a month or a semester on each one, and you will see a big improvement quickly.

So what does your new high school student need to know? What should middle school parents be doing now to give teens a strong start? Here is a checklist of goals I use with my middle school students to make sure they are well-prepared before high school begins.

Get ready for high school.

Read independently

Not all homeschool students love to read; half of mine love it, and half of them hate it. So as much as we want to instill a love of good books into our students—

and continue saturating them with quality reading material and good read-aloud time—a serious book addiction won't strike all of them. Sorry to burst your bubble.

Yet, every high school student needs to be able to get the job done: finish reading assignments in a timely manner with good comprehension and quickly skim for needed information. If students can read, at-or-above grade level (and even glean facts from more difficult books as necessary), and answer thoughtful questions on the author's message and intent, the job is done. No one said they have to like it.

If a student has reading difficulties, is unable to recall what is read a day or two later, and cannot research a topic from multiple sources, he may benefit from working on these skills with another year of middle school before beginning high school studies.

Understand basic math

Math skills vary wildly in the teen years. Asking "where should my student be in math?" is a lot like saying, "how good a piano player should my teen be?" There are too many variables:

- What's his ability?
- How often does he practice?
- Does the family have a strong aptitude or culture of enjoying the subject?
- Does he love it?
- Is he in a learning plateau or on the verge of a big mental growth spurt?

I'll be spending more time on the subject of math later in chapter 10. However, for middle school, there are two important points, one for you and one for the student.

First of all, the student needs to understand the basics of math -- addition, subtraction, multiplication, and division. He needs to understand what these functions mean and how they are related to each other and how to express them both by using words and with numbers and even in real-life stories. He needs to understand how to express math equations using whole things and parts of things (fractions and decimals). He needs to understand how to measure real items (from pencils to fields of grass to money) in a variety of forms and how to translate the answers to different units of measurement. Finally, he needs to practice doing mental math (what he will use most in his everyday life), and he needs to demonstrate how to show his work on paper when working complicated problems. He needs a lot of experiential knowledge with math in the real world so he is comfortable using it and understanding it.

Secondly, you as the parent need to understand where your student is with his math skills and where he's likely to go with math. You may not have thought about this much if your math curriculum basically consists of "do the next worksheet." That is just fine, we just need to start paying attention over the next few weeks or months. Does he finish his math quickly and easily with little or no help from you, or does it feel like a foreign language to him? Does he do math in his head during the day, like estimating how much sales tax he needs for a purchase or how many miles he has traveled in 20 minutes while riding in a car

28

driving 35 miles per hour (yes, some students find this weirdly fun)? Has he started algebra, and is that fun or maddening for him? How comfortable is he with rearranging equations of unknown quantities or imagining shapes rotating in space? These are all clues as to how prepared your child is mentally for algebra and geometry. By considering his mental capabilities, you can better plan for the future and pace his math in a way that reduces frustrations for you both.

In other words, do not expect your student will follow the exact same math progress as your homeschool friend across town. Your student may speed through calculus and statistics, or he may draw out algebra and geometry. What is most important is that you discern his natural mathematical pace and adjust his curriculum accordingly.

Write a strong paragraph

High school requires essays and research papers, so middle school students should already understand paragraph form. Take the time (or even an entire course) to teach students how to write complete

29

sentences and how to recognize and correct fragments and run-ons. Then explain how to construct a simple paragraph with a topic sentence, strong body, and conclusion. Then finally, show him how to put the assignment away and check it the next day for grammar, spelling, and content errors to produce a flawless final copy. This skill will improve the student's confidence and even grades in every single subject.

Manage time responsibly

I put these two ideas of **responsibility** and **time management** together because, for preteens and teens, they really go hand in hand. Students are not responsible for much more than how they use their time because that is the basis of their day. Are they spending time on their studies or daydreaming? Are they practicing their musical instruments or YouTubing? Are they finishing their chores or picking arguments with their siblings? It is all about how they use their time.

When our children were little, most of us used chore charts to teach our children daily habits. Now is the time to train our middle school students how to use a planner or notebook to organize their work. At first, I write a weekly list of what needs to be accomplished, and I will check it every day, then every couple of days, and later just weekly. Students know there will be consequences for "smiling or having fun of any kind" before the responsibilities are finished (I sound like a work Nazi because my homeschool children think it is always happy playtime if I do not crack down). By the time a student begins high school, he should be able to manage all his own chores, jobs, projects, assignments, and personal appointments without reminders or nagging from parents. That is the goal, anyway.

Maximize his learning style

While working on all those academic skills, the student will soon realize he prefers to do things a certain way:

- He studies better in the morning, or he prefers the afternoon.
- He likes music playing when he does his math, or he needs silence.

- He remembers new concepts if he discusses them with a parent, or he memorizes better if he reads.

- Projects make him happy, or he dreads anything that requires crafting.

As parents, we can begin taking a step back from directing every detail of each assignment during the middle school years. As we move away from micromanaging our student's learning, our preteen becomes freer to learn as he does best—using his unique learning style to its fullest potential.

Are you intrigued? Stay tuned. In chapter 5, I will explain how to identify your student's learning style and your own teaching style. Then we will see how both of those can work together to make homeschooling high school even easier.

Study for a test

Whether or not you keep track of grades for elementary and middle school assignments (I mostly don't), high school needs those letters and numbers on the transcript. The best way to help students prepare for those high school tests is by practicing in middle school. Many classes lend themselves well to testing, especially history, science, and math. Guide your student through the process for a year or two, and then back off and let him prepare on his own. Middle school students need to practice studying over time (instead of cramming), taking notes, memorizing facts, and presenting their knowledge on paper in an essay, short answer, and multiple-choice formats. For many homeschoolers, these skills need quite a bit of practice.

How do you teach a homeschool student study skills? If the student has been homeschooled his entire life, this can be a little more challenging. Tailor-made or eclectic homeschool curriculum create a wonderful learning culture for young students, but sometimes leave students unprepared to buckle down and test well. Here are some pointers that have helped my students in this area:

1. Test regularly

By middle school years, your student should be regularly practicing test-taking, whether or not you are keeping a long-term record of his grades. Simply taking tests and observing his grades will help students understand how much effort it takes to do well.

2. Require memorization

Elementary students face a variety of information to memorize verses, math facts, state capitals, presidents, being verbs. Keep requiring middle school students to memorize lists and facts and dates and places to continue building those brain muscles.

3. Teach note-taking.

Every week, we hold a family-wide history discussion. Every student, regardless of his grade level, participates according to his ability. The middle school students and high school students bring paper and pencil to take notes. At first, students need prompting (write this down!). But gradually they begin to understand what verbal cues show important points, phrases like "these three issues . . ." or "the most important factor in the war . . ." or "the five most significant contributions are . . ."

Another great note-taking opportunity is church. Students who practice taking sermon notes become familiar with outline form, supporting references, and examples.

4. Coach before tests.

To a certain extent, middle school students need to be taught to the test. They need us to tell them what information is most important to focus on. After a few years, they will develop better instincts for prioritizing their study time.

Even though we don't gear our lessons toward the test, we still want to leave some time for pre-test coaching. Look over the quiz and give the student ideas what kind of questions will be given: are they multiple choice, short answer, or essay? Clue them in on what material is covered: is it primarily from one resource, skill, or perspective? Point out how he has already prepared: are the test questions taken from the class discussion, worksheets, or activities?

5. Train him in specific strategies.

A few students need little help learning how to study; they instinctively understand what they need to do and prepare themselves well. Most preteens are *not* like that.

This is why you will have to guide your preteen through some of the study practices that to *you* may seem obvious. When grades don't improve, you may even need to require some of these activities:

- Creating flash cards
- Memorizing all bold-faced words
- Memorizing worksheet answers
- Creating fill-in-the-blank study guide
- Asking a friend or family member to quiz him
- Covering up notes and reciting them aloud, revealing one line of information at a time to check his work.

6. Keep practicing.

Study skills will not dawn upon your student instantaneously. Like all other pursuits, he will fail several times before getting the hang of it. However, with continued practice, your preteen will soon understand what the word *study* means and how to succeed in difficult subjects.

Is your student ready for high school?

Here's the my high-school readiness checklist:

- ☐ Read at or above grade level
- ☐ Read with comprehension of the facts presented
- ☐ Read for specific information
- ☐ Understand how to add, subtract, multiply, and divide multiply two- and three-digit numbers without a calculator
- ☐ Understand how to add, subtract, multiply, and divide fractions and decimal numbers
- ☐ Understand how to convert fractions to decimals to percent
- ☐ Understand the relationship between addition and subtraction and between multiplication and division
- ☐ Solve multi-step story problems involving addition, subtraction, multiplication, and division, and even

create his own story about given problems

☐ Demonstrate the real-world application of his math studies

☐ Able to convert units of measurement (feet to inches, meters to yards, pounds to grams, etc.)

☐ Practice with solving for area, perimeter, and volume of polygons and circles

☐ Begin working with unknown quantities (solving for x)

☐ Solving for ratios and rates (miles per hour)

☐ Estimating

☐ Studying for tests and practicing multiple methods of test preparation

☐ Taking notes from fill-in-the-blank and outline

☐ Writing an essay paragraph on a given topic

☐ Writing a paragraph on steps to a procedure

☐ Writing a persuasive paragraph

☐ Keeps track of assignments and responsibilities with little oversight

☐ Knows his favorite learning style and how to use it

☐ Develop personal strategies for learning in styles he *does not* enjoy when necessary

☐ _____

_____

☐ _____

_____

☐ _____

_____

☐ _____

_____

☐ _____

_____

☐ _____

_____

☐ _____

_____

3. High School Year by Year

The new year stands before us, like a chapter in a book, waiting to be written. We can help write that story by setting goals.
-- Melody Beattie

THERE ARE ONLY FOUR SHORT YEARS in high school. Trust me when I say they go by really, really fast. Like, blink-of-an-eye fast. Faster than you can drink a pot of coffee. Faster than your teen can scatter clothes and books around a clean house. Faster than you can lose your minivan keys. So, really fast, in other words.

When I first started homeschooling high school, I wish I had a big-picture-overview of what the four years of high school would bring. The big picture would have saved me quite a bit of stress and nagging and anxiety. Now that I have homeschooled the high school years for several years, I realize that there is a pattern here, a nice set of steps between "oh my word, this is FUR REALS!" and "Wow. It's over already?"

Before we get deep into all the nitty-gritty of homeschooling high school, including each subject and requirement and transcript and life skill, I thought I would whisper some soothing words of big-picture-planning into your ear. Because that is ever so comforting, isn't it? Not sure you agree? Read on, and see if this does not make you feel better about high school than you ever imagined.

Freshman Year

Ninth grade is a big step from middle school to the scary high school (insert Hitchcock soundtrack here). This year you and your student progress from that frozen-in-the-headlights state of paralyzing fear to the confident "we got this" swagger of homeschool high school pros. It will happen, I guarantee . . . just wait for it.

In the meantime, while you are waiting, help your student accomplish these goals (one at a time, not all at once, unless your name is Lea Ann the Crazy):

- Become increasingly independent in study skills
- Manage schoolwork and time
- Identify how, where, and when he learns best
- Research your state graduation requirements and plan a general high school course accordingly
- Ensure completion of core classes (English, math, science, history) and any electives
- Track grades and have that "oh no, this is harder than we thought" moment or two
- Try an extra-curricular (sports, music, etc.) or two or several, then freak out over how busy and overcommitted you are and pare down
- Make friends at church and get involved with a local ministry
- Have a few heart-to-heart discussions between both parents and the student about balancing school work, extracurricular activities, ministry, household chores, friends, and video game time

Sophomore Year

Tenth grade is perhaps the best year of high school. The student has hopefully experienced a spiritual revival toward the end of freshman year about being responsible (all the praise hands) and has a more realistic expectation of high school work. He has probably streamlined his studying and academics to just what he needs to get the job done, and he is more realistic about how well prepared he needs to become for tests and projects. He has high school under control and may be ready to take on even more responsibility.

So if the freshman year ended well, the sophomore year should be just building on success. Here are some tips to make the most of this year:

- Let the student take charge of his academic plan. Schedule a regular end-of-the-week meeting to report on progress and take tests. No more micro managing unless he begins missing deadlines.

- If there is an elective he wants to try out, this is the year to do it.

- Check those state requirements again to determine if your student will graduate with minimum, standard, or distinguished achievement (advanced) program. Often you will find a considerable difference in requirements for each level. For examples of the difference, google "YOUR STATE graduation requirements."

- Teach your student to track his own grades and understand the future financial implications of his grade point average (scholarships!).

- Encourage your student to begin a list of possible careers, college majors, and schools he finds interesting. Don't put pressure on this, just encourage him to start fact-gathering and dreaming.

- Fulfill that sport or PE requirement, if he has not done so already.

- Volunteer in a ministry at church (nursery, choir, children's Sunday School, etc.).

- Begin a part-time job outside the home and take on some part of his own financial responsibilities (buying his own entertainment, clothes, electronics, etc.).

Junior Year

I am going to tell you the truth: the junior year is the hardest. The student completes *so much* and makes big strides toward leaving home during eleventh grade. It is good to start these final steps steps now so that if real life or mistakes or unforeseen circumstances get in the way, the student has another year to fall back on.

After the relative ease of the sophomore year, you may (like me) be tempted to go back to micromanaging and nagging to make sure that these things get done. Fight the urge and let your student learn from consequences; he would do well to learn these lessons now than when he is thirty years old, right?

- Let the student plan the junior year more, selecting from available curriculum and classes that meet his graduation requirements. You may even let him plan his school calendar, including the end of semester dates and due dates. Ask him how much or little reminder he wants. This is important preparation for college and career.

- Focus on core required courses to prepare for college entrance tests; save easy, fluff, and elective courses for senior year (when neither one of you will be caring as much anymore, anyway).

- Have the student narrow his list of potential majors to two or three, and make a list of three to five schools he is interested in attending.

- Take sample ACT and SAT tests to find which one fits your student best. Register for a test date (preferably spring of junior year) and get started preparing.

- Take the student to visit some colleges and have him contact admissions departments for more information. Encourage the student to take the lead on college decisions and communication with admissions officers and college faculty himself; this makes a strong impression.

- Find out your state requirements for a driver's license and begin that process. Encourage the student to save up for his own vehicle, insurance, and maintenance, or perhaps pay his parents for use of the family vehicle. This helps ensure responsible management of both finances and vehicles.

- Prioritize ministry and volunteering to keep the student others-focused during an intense period of self-care and growth.

Senior Year

After the past three years of hard work, this should be the gravy year. If your student did, indeed, complete all of the above junior year goals, he is now working part-time, driving his own car, paying some of his own bills, communicating regularly with his favorite college, and honing in on his future career and ministry. He is quite busy and almost an adult . . . seemingly overnight.

However, most students cannot get *all* of those junior year goals completed in one year. So during his senior year, the student can pick up the rest, checking off his steps toward independence.

- Finish graduation requirements that remain undone. He may have completed his state's minimum requirements as a junior. Continue encouraging him to finish the year strong for better chances for college admission and scholarships.
- Finalize his plans for college: if he's going to college, where he will attend, what he will study, and how he will pay for it.
- Retake his college entrance exams, if desired.
- Submit his applications to his college(s) of choice and follow the steps to admissions they provide.
- If the academic workload is light, increase working outside the home to full-time. Take on more financial responsibility and save aggressively for college costs.
- Once he has secured college admittance, begin paying tuition.
- Apply for scholarships outside the college.

49

- Continue volunteering in the church and community. Take initiative to fill needs instead of saying, "Someone should . . . "
- Discuss among both parents and student what changes (and what stays the same) as the teen transitions to an adult member of the family.

Does that seem like a lot? It does look overwhelming if you take the entire list, look at your thirteen-year-old, and try to imagine cramming all of that into him. It will not work, obviously. So do not even try.

Take this just a year at a time. Some years (like tenth grade) seem like a piece of cake. Others (I hate you, eleventh grade!) have a lot of change and pressure. Instead of stressing over high school, take each year at a time, a goal at a time, a life lesson at a time, a prayer at a time.

Yes, homeschooling high school can sometimes seem overwhelming. Yet in reality, this too *can* be easy -- one day at a time.

4. Your Teaching Style Made Easy

Tell me and I forget. Teach me and I remember.
Involve me and I learn.
-- Benjamin Franklin

I SPENT A LOT OF TIME in *Homeschool Made Easy* explaining how to find your teaching style and how to identify your student's learning style. These two concepts are separate. Your **teaching style** describes the way you communicate with your children, the style of teaching you naturally gravitate toward, and the materials you find easiest to use. You may be a hands-on, crafty, creative mom who dreams of dioramas and lapbooks and who starts every lesson with "let's go to Hobby Lobby for more glitter!" If so, you are nothing like me. I am an avid book collector who easily lapses into lecturing and waving my hands in the air to magically waft knowledge into small brains, and I'd love to start every lesson with "let's go to the museum!"

Often times our homeschool angst comes from watching other moms at the co-op (or stalking them on Pinterest) and beating ourselves up for not homeschooling like they do. Sister, *you aren't me* and *I ain't you,* and neither one of us should be teaching our children the exact same way. We have different skills, talents, personalities, and backgrounds that lend themselves to teaching different ways. "You do *your* homeschool," to borrow a popular cliché.

The same principle holds true of our students. They each have their own way of approaching new problems (and all of learning is a new problem!). Rarely should we force a student to learn a standardized way. Instead, if we can help him find his best way of tackling new subjects, we can give our student a valuable problem-solving tool *for the rest of his life!*

So if like me, you love Venn diagrams, you can imagine a big circle of your teaching style and another big circle of your student's learning style. Right in the middle where those two circles overlap reveals that yummy, beautiful sweet spot that reveals your family's unique learning culture. This is where you want to live Monday through Friday, if at all possible.

Ok, so how to find that special little bubble of beauty, that magical wonderland of teaching and learning awesomeness that is the intersection of your teaching style and your student's learning style? Let's start with you.

Homeschool Teaching Styles

Up to this point, you may or may not have been very conscious of your teaching style. So take a moment to pay attention to what how you best teach.

In **traditional classroom** learning, there are many different recognized teaching styles. The common styles include *authoritative* (tell them), *demonstrative* (show them), *facilitative* (clear a path for them), and *delegative* (answer them). But homeschooling, a primarily one-on-one educational model, has developed different teaching styles: *traditional, Charlotte Mason, classical, unschooling, eclectic.* Most homeschoolers are more familiar with a few of these more popular styles, though there are myriads more.

Most homeschool families will experiment with several different styles before settling on a hybrid of teaching methods that fit their own family best. I know I sure did. We were very traditional at first, then we morphed into Charlotte Mason and nearly unschooled before settling into a loose classical style. Many high school homeschoolers are very passionate about their way of doing high school. Their co-op, their online class, their curriculum, their CLEP classes, their dual credit courses are the only way to go – *for them*. Remember that as you smile and nod and say, "I'm so happy you found a great plan for you!"

Remember, **homeschooling is easy when we prioritize our focus (love God, love others) and communicate this the way God uniquely enables us. Find your *why* and communicate it *your way*.** Don't ever feel pressured that any one style is better than another or that there is one right way of teaching your child. God disciples each of us personally, doesn't He? Whatever method(s) fit your family culture best, use that to the best of your ability. With confidence. And coffee. Lots of coffee.

Traditional/textbook

This is your style if you want your lesson plans already laid out for you, scripted, with matching worksheets and pre-made tests and answer keys. No matter what your homeschool style from preschool through middle school, you are likely to use traditional textbook method for at least some of high school.

This style seems to have a bad reputation with many homeschoolers, but that's their hang-up, not yours. Use what works for you. You will likely feel more confident teaching with traditional textbooks if you need that list of things to do each day to feel like you are homeschooling right, or if you prefer to hand something to your teen and let him manage his own academics.

Make it easy: Micro-manage his assignments less and less after his freshman year, noticing how well he performs. By sophomore or junior year, you should be able to simply tell him when his tests will be given and let him decide how much studying he will do and how he will do it. Remember that mastery of the material (and the grades to prove it) is the goal for high school, *not completing every question or example.* If that helps him learn, then great. But if he just needs to work through a little bit and he has it, then more power to him!

By junior or senior year, your student may be responsible enough to plan out his own course entirely. Tell him when you have scheduled the course deadline for his final grade, then let him tell you when to give him each test. That way he could even finish early if he wishes!

Key thought: Let the student customize his own course and even deadlines.

Unschooling

This is your style if you believe in letting your student choose his educational path, letting his natural curiosity ignite his love for learning. Sometimes called delight-directed learning or even child-led learning, this style is characterized by a lack of curriculum, plan, or structure.

This is the only style of teaching, quite frankly, which causes me a problem. This is a philosophical issue: I firmly believe it is the parent's responsibility to guide, direct, and train the child, not vice versa. However, I have personally followed a quasi-unschooled approach during periods of family stress and serious illness. And still, we didn't immediately get struck by lightning. Also, if there is ever a time to lean toward unschooling, the early years is the time. Unschoolers have the edge on making learning fun, natural, and organic to their daily lives, which is the entire purpose of the early learning years. Therefore, there is something for all of us to learn from unschooling. Many unschoolers switch to more traditional textbooks for high school in order to give a more objective measurement of mastery.

If you are an unschooler, now is time to tighten up your educational plan. How are you going to document and measure learning for high school? What proof of achievement can you show colleges and employers? What standards will you use for each course completion and for graduation?

If you are transitioning to a more traditional or textbook standard of education for high school, most of that will be covered for you. Just be aware that these are big changes for your student so you can help him adjust.

Even if you wish to remain unschooling through graduation, your student's college plans may affect your courses. If he wishes to pursue higher education, this is a great time for you to help him learn what his professors will expect of him in the classroom (or online courses). Help him master test taking, essays, and research reports, and make him turn in projects on deadlines. He needs to become accustomed to documenting how and what he has learned.

58

Make it easy: If you did not begin transitioning toward textbooks during middle school, be aware of the difficulties your high school freshman may experience adjusting to the new style. Help him develop study skills early so he can enjoy more independence later in high school.

Key thought: Plan, measure, and document.

Charlotte Mason and Classical

If you know what a *real book* is (and your bookshelves are full of them), you prize discipline as a necessary virtue, and you practice *narration*, you are **Charlotte Mason**. Ok, maybe Charlotte is not your name, but you are a follower of her teaching methods. The Charlotte Mason style encourages gentle teaching for the early years with a careful eye toward character development and communication. What's not to love?

If you yearn to synchronize the humanities together -- history, literature, writing, the arts -- and study them as a whole, if the answer to every question is a history lesson, if you love drawing connections

59

through your subjects across the span of time, if the idea of teaching all your children together in four-year cycles of world studies makes your heart flutter, then you are likely a **classical** homeschooler. With *or without* the Latin classes.

By high school, Charlotte Mason students very closely resemble relaxed classical teens, so I've grouped them together. High school studies are rewarding for all these students. At last, after years of working hard to memorize facts and outlining events in their timelines, these students can put together all the lessons they have been learning, examine the unified themes running through all their subjects, and communicate their own carefully considered beliefs. They begin applying the lessons from the past to the challenges of the present. They are more articulate and mature in their thinking, so discussions are thought-provoking and interesting.

If you have been teaching in a classical or Charlotte Mason style for a few years, your teen has likely been moving toward independent learning since middle school. In that case, the transition to high school should not be very difficult. The hard part will be tackling weightier subject matter, heavier reading, and longer writing assignments. But, hey, that's his problem, not yours! ha!

By this point, you should be able to meet with your student for about one or two hours once a week for each subject. Beyond that, he should be preparing for each class time with you by completing a week's worth of assignments, including reading and writing assignments. So your job is just to help him with corrections and to keep him going in the right direction.

Make it easy: Sit down with your teen before the academic year starts to discuss each subject -- what will be required, what resources he will use, and how the grades will be determined. Work together on a schedule for class times, when you will meet together for discussion, correction, and tests. Then hold him accountable for being prepared for each class.

Key thought: Let him take charge of his learning.

Eclectic

Maybe you cannot describe your homeschooling with one style because you take ideas from several different methods for your own. I personally am several different styles, depending on the subject matter. We are relaxed classical for the humanities and fairly textbook for the sciences. The longer you homeschool, the more comfortable you will be **making your homeschool style your own.** That is the secret to success in anything.

The key to high school success is simple:

- let your student take responsibility for his learning
- find objective measurements for grading each class
- document his learning
- hold him responsible with painfully honest grades

Keep it simple: Remember that at this point *your teen is responsible for his own grades, not you.* It is hard not to take his failings personally, but his failures are so important to his own learning. Don't get in the way of that. Dock his paper for being late. Use a consistent rubric for grading his papers. Let him know how his grades are averaging out so he can work to bring them up.

Key thought: Let your student earn his grades.

5. High School Learning Styles

"If a child can't learn the way we teach, maybe we should teach the way they learn."
— Ignacio Estrada

LET'S TAKE A CLOSER LOOK at *learning styles*. The discussion of learning styles either simplifies things for you or makes you feel guilty. I used to be in the latter camp. My gut reaction to learning style theory was to feel anxious that I was not properly igniting my child's passion in his own educational language. You know that fear, that *I'm not teaching right* feeling. But that's just not the truth.

Instead, *learning style theory* should empower us – and our students – to **learn the way they learn**

best. The basic idea of learning styles is that everyone gravitates toward one or two ways to learn new things, strategies that help us understand and utilize new information easily. This is one of many educational models; there are other ways of looking at how we learn. But this is one model that is easy for both teachers and students to understand, so it is popular for homeschoolers to use to learning styles to describe how they overcome learning roadblocks. My favorite book on learning styles is *They Way They Learn* by Cynthia Ulrich Tobias.

There are three basic learning styles: visual, auditory, and kinesthetic. In a nutshell, *visual learners* learn by reading, looking at diagrams, and even writing what they are thinking about. They learn by seeing. Non-verbal communication is very important to visual learners (I have a hard time talking on the phone because I'm such a visual learner!). *Auditory learners* prefer to listen, discuss, and recite as an aid to understanding and memorization. They learn by hearing. Finally, kinesthetic learners (as well as most teen boys who drive their mothers crazy) learn with hands-on experiments, making messes, trial-and-error, and anything that involves not thinking ahead to the consequences. They learn by doing.

If you have more than one kinesthetic learner in your house, I will add you to my daily prayer list. If you are a kinesthetic learner yourself, I love you very much, but I cannot understand anything about you (yes, dear husband, I am looking at you).

Now, learning styles should be a blessing when we don't use them to berate ourselves for not teaching to our student's favorite style every day. That was my hang-up; please don't adopt it as yours. Instead, we should be empowered that our teen *can* find an avenue for loving learning.

Whether your student recognizes his learning style or not, you will need to help your teen figure out how to tackle difficult high school subjects. You want to teach your student so much more than simply *how to survive this one assignment* or even *how to ace this test*. The more important lessons are *how to endure difficult courses, how to apply challenging material,* and *how to learn independently.* Those are the lessons that will last a lifetime.

So while you may be giving gentle reminders and encouragement to your high school freshman, by the senior year your student should be applying his own learning style and studying on his own successfully.

Here are some ways many high school students and even adults apply their learning style independently:

Visual

- research and study at the library
- collect a personal library of resources
- google for more information and illustrations
- subscribe to industry magazines
- take notes during lectures to retain more information
- read and study alone, asking questions only when necessary

Auditory

- attend lecture or discussion to learn new information
- listen to audio books
- join a performance group
- seek out professionals and other trusted advisors for help
- repeat/recite new information to internalize it

Kinesthetic

- walk, jog, or bounce a ball while thinking about new concepts
- spread out supplies, materials, and resources while learning
- create hands-on projects or experiments to test knowledge and application
- create reminders, routines, and sensory triggers to remember important tasks or information

Many kinesthetic learners enter high school and college thinking they are worse students than their peers are. *This is a grave error.* While many high school and college courses are designed to maximize the natural strengths of auditory and visual learners, *kinesthetic students win every time at application.* This fact is not intuitively obvious to students, however, and they need more encouragement to find their edge. The truth is that **adulthood is about applying what you know.** Encourage your teen to put into practice everything he learns as quickly as possible, whether that is tutoring, helping younger siblings with their work, presenting mini-reports, completing projects, volunteering in the community, or even getting a job. As he sees his success putting his education to work, he will be motivated to continue doing his best.

6. Scheduling a Typical Day

Success is no accident. It is hard work, perseverance,
learning, studying, sacrifice and most of all, love of
what you are doing or learning to do.

-- Pele

THERE IS NO SUCH THING as a "typical homeschooler" any more than there is such thing as a "normal day." Are you normal? I don't have to tell you that I'm not!

Yet when my children were approaching middle school, I wondered what a typical day of high school homeschooling would look like for us. How would we finish all that work? How much would my student do on his own? How would we cram sports and music and ministry and work into our already-packed-full family calendar? *Would I lose my mind?*

Ok, the answer to the last question is "yes," but not because of homeschooling. I'm just nuts. You don't *have* to be nuts to homeschool high school, but it helps explain the madness to others.

Anyway, after some trial and error, missteps and adjustments, we have settled into a nice routine for our high school years. We worked out a lot of kinks with my oldest (now graduated), and my daughter is making this homeschool high school life all her own.

So to help you imagine how a busy family manages it all through the teen years, I thought I would share with you a "typical" week (whatever that is!) from my perspective *and* from Adana, our current high schooler. She is in 10th grade this year and studying classically as well as from textbooks. She is primarily a visual learner, though she enjoys some auditory activities (especially discussion). On top of her homeschooling, she plays soccer, performs in a local orchestra, works part time, and teaches Cubbies in her church's AWANA program. She is currently interested in pursuing a college degree in education or writing.

Adana is taking the following subjects:

Bible AWANA Journey curriculum, church history (Tapestry of Grace, Year 3)

English Jensen Grammar, Jensen Vocabulary, Tapestry of Grace Literature Lite (online discussion through Lampstand Bookshelf)

History Tapestry of Grace Year 3, rhetoric level with extra reading

Math Saxon's *Algebra 2*

Science Jay Wile's *Exploring Creation with Chemistry*

Music private piano and violin from me, church music ministry, orchestra

PE club soccer

Monday

Each weekday, I set my alarm for 6 am for devotions, journaling, and reading before everyone wakes up. My children and teens make their own breakfast, clean their rooms, and do a few household chores before we start studies. We should begin Bible time between 8 and 9 in the morning. Today is my youngest child's turn to do his laundry, so he starts a load before we begin.

After we read and discuss from the *Illustrated Family Bible Stories* or *A Family Guide to Narnia*, we have another group lesson on geography, music history, art appreciation, or church history. Today the youngest reads aloud from the *Passport to the World* about Bolivia since we are studying South American history this month.

It is the beginning of the new week, so everyone gets out their assignment notebooks. I fill in assignments and due dates for the two younger boys while Adana writes down her own goals for the week.

On Mondays, I teach language arts to everyone. Adana and Leandro (8th grade) are both doing *Jensen's Vocabulary* together. She helps him match the words and definitions for the new list of terms this week. Then I hand her the grading book for her *Jensen's Grammar*, and she checks last week's homework herself. When she is ready, I give her this week's test and grade it quickly. She then moves on to study other

74

subjects while I finish English lessons with the other students.

Before lunch, we practice singing. The three of them are learning a special song for church, and Adana and I are rehearsing a duet for next month. Then we each make our own meal, and I read aloud from *Of Courage Undaunted.*

After lunch every day, everyone works quietly. I write for a couple hours, the boys do homework by moving to a different room or flat surface every 15 minutes. Adana studies quietly in her room then practices the violin and piano and does her Spanish.

Early evening, we work together on house chores. Mondays we pick up the downstairs clutter, vacuum, and dust. Adana finishes supper preparations for me while I greet David when he walks in. We all sit down to dinner around 5:30.

I visit with David for a few minutes after supper before he takes Adana to soccer practice. The boys play with their friends, and I practice the violin. Everyone is in bed shortly after 9:30.

Tuesday

The day starts the same way, but now we are looking at math. Adana works on her geometry on her own and plans to take a test Friday. We eat lunch a little sooner because she has an online literature discussion at 12:30 for 90 minutes. For the rest of the afternoon, she finishes some work in vocabulary, geometry, and grammar then studies her chemistry and practices. After supper, she has soccer practice again.

Wednesday

This is the day Adana works tending shop for a seamstress. After our morning lessons, she packs a backpack with just about every textbook she owns, as well as snacks and lunch. I drop her off for several hours, and she completes much of her homework for the rest of the week while waiting for customers.

She finishes geometry work and completes the rest of the vocabulary and grammar homework for the week. Then she reads chemistry and completes the study guide questions and studies for her upcoming test. She completes her AWANA work that remains for the week. Finally, she reads her history assignments, which includes biographies and history books from the early 19th century.

After I bring her home from work, Adana puts her school books away and cooks dinner for the family. We eat early, and then David takes all of the children to AWANA. Adana teaches Cubbies and says her own verses.

Thursday

After our morning time together, I have history discussion with all the students for an hour or two. We discuss the week's readings and the historical events covered. Our discussions cover not only history but also worldview, philosophy, church history, geography, and art history. We finish up a little before lunchtime. Because Adana has finished so much during work Wednesday, this is a light day for her. She will finish any remaining written work like church history now, study for her upcoming history test, and then practice her instruments.

Thursday afternoons we often schedule field trips to local art museums, zoos, or cultural events. After dinner Thursday evening, Adana and I play in a two-hour orchestra rehearsal.

Friday

Friday is a test day. I make sure the younger students have completed their assignments and projects for the week, but Adana is more self-directed. Usually, she will have a couple tests for me to proctor and grade. She normally finishes before lunch. In the afternoon and evening, she likes to go running, do some babysitting, or watch a classic movie marathon with her younger brother.

So while Adana is a very busy teen, homeschooling helps her make the most of her time. While helping me document her typical week, she remarked that she does more than she thought; the work just seems manageable because she's in control of her time.

7. The Pros and Cons of Homeschool Classes

It is the supreme art of the teacher to awaken joy in creative expression and knowledge.

-- Albert Einstein

WELL, IT'S TIME to finally talk about something controversial: **classes for homeschool teens.** We have all heard quite a bit about what kinds of classes are available for homeschoolers, how to make the most of the group opportunities, and even how to earn college credit with high school courses. Yet I do not see people talking about the basic question we need to consider first: *why should homeschool students take these classes?*

When we stop and think about it, we *are* homeschoolers, right? That means we decided for one reason or another to remove our students from

79

the traditional classroom and educate them counter-culturally. We chose to focus on the needs and abilities of our individual child, providing customized, one-on-one teaching for communicating our own homeschool *why*. Yet during the high school years, we suddenly change course, looking for ways to put them back *into* a class. That seems, at first glance, counter-purpose.

Stay with me here. I may not be concluding the way you imagine. Actually, you might understand this entire chapter better if you remember what we discussed in chapter one.

A big push during the high school years of homeschooling is *dual credit*, the opportunity for high school students to earn college credit while taking the very same high school courses required for graduation. This means that as high school students, our teens can take college courses at the local community college. Classes taught by secular instructors in secular classrooms filled with secular young adults. This is where many homeschool families send their 14, 15, and 16-year-olds.

Even those of us who would never send our teens to public schools.

The entire idea is super tempting. When my oldest son was in middle school, I had every intention of dual-crediting him all the way through high school. Who wouldn't want their 17-year-old to graduate from high school and college – BAM – all at the same time? That would be so totally awesome! As a homeschooled teen who graduated a year early just to prove I could do it, dual credit sounded like a challenge with my name written all over it.

Then life happened. My son turned fourteen, high school rolled around, and he had no desire whatsoever to accelerate his learning. Actually, getting the bare minimum done was more than he aspired to (teens! go figure!). What's more, neither he nor I felt like he was mature enough to handle college-level coursework.

The more my husband and I thought about it, we found another concern. I had met enough homeschool graduates to know that young men who had never learned outside their own four walls faced another big

81

temptation -- **intellectual arrogance**. After learning and achieving so much independently, it is tempting for homeschoolers to believe *I can do all things because I am just smarter than the average bear* rather than to rely on the Lord. We wanted our teens to learn mental humility – the ability to learn from others, the understanding that one person can't know it all, and the submission to follow instructions, formats, and requirements of other teachers.

To tell you the truth, I was just plain tired. Let's be honest, homeschooling several children at once can wear a mother out. When puberty starts for more than one of them, mom is about done in. Pray for the homeschool mom near you.

So for all those reasons, I told my husband it was probably time to put our son into a couple of classes. Classes taught by teachers that supported our own homeschool *why* while delivering academic excellence in a college-preparatory curriculum. David was all for this from the beginning, but we still discussed the matter carefully to make sure we knew *why* we were making this decision and how it lined up with our family values:

- to support our family's educational values (teaching them to love God, love others, and work hard),
- to teach the student how to learn from teachers not related to him by blood,
- to prepare him mentally for the rigors of college ahead, and
- to give new insights, new understanding, new opportunities not available from my teaching.

Once we had those priorities clarified, it was immediately clear what classes we would choose. I wanted to enroll my student into an online discussion with a good literature teacher that used our same curriculum (Tapestry of Grace) that provides the framework for all our humanities studies. I found the publisher offered online classes that utilized discussion in a small group to reinforce the literary principles he would be learning. His teacher would grade him on his participation in class (and that teacher was a tough grader! He had to offer detailed analysis every week) and on his power point presentations to the group (another opportunity I couldn't provide at home).

My son also asked if he could take science classes online from a "real scientist." So, I found science classes that he took for three years online. This was his hardest class each year, and he learned a lot.

If we make sure we knew *why* we are homeschooling, we will know how to line everything else up with our family values, even group classes.

As I customize our curriculum for each of our students, our daughter is taking one online class: that same literature course. After taking science online last year and discovering she is more of a visual than an auditory learner, she opted to study on her own (and she is actually doing better). She does have a desire to take dual credit courses at some point, but her father and I have pointed out these points above, that for high school, every opportunity she takes needs to fit with our family's homeschool *why*. In that case, dual credit at the local community college does not support our family's values, so that would be a step backward, away from our homeschool *why*. She is considering obtaining dual credit online through an accredited Christian institution in the near future, instead.

Now, here is the bottom line: *most of my friends do not completely agree with me on the issue of homeschool high school classes.* All the homeschool mommies I know use a combination of online and co-ops and dual credit, and they are very happy with their decision. I do not stand in judgment over them because, quite frankly, I am too busy chasing my own tail over here. I even have friends who run their own co-ops. More power to them. In most of those cases, I know those moms have found classes and educational opportunities that support their own homeschool *why*. That, my friend, is the entire point.

No one's homeschool *why* will completely match mine, so no one's homeschool will look just like mine. We all make different decisions for our teens. You homeschool your way because that's how you homeschool best.

If you are weighing the pros and cons of homeschool high school classes, pray over these things for a bit. Then sit down with your husband over a burrito bowl and bag of chips and talk through your family's *why,* the priorities that drive your homeschool forward. Together, you will find the solution that fits your family best.

8. History and Bible

My son, if you receive my words
and treasure up my commandments with you,
making your ear attentive to wisdom
and inclining your heart to understanding;
yes, if you call out for insight
and raise your voice for understanding,
if you seek it like silver
and search for it as for hidden treasures,
then you will understand the fear of the Lord
and find the knowledge of God.
-- Proverbs 2:1-5

TWO ACADEMIC COURSES set the foundation for all the rest of our studies in the Garfias home. These two disciplines shape the emphasis for the rest of our classes, they fuel our family discussions around the dinner table, they inspire our family vacation destinations, and (we pray) they shape the adults our young people will become. These two all-important classes are **Bible and history.**

Bible and history form the core of our homeschool. These two subjects intertwine quite a bit, too. We cannot discuss history without noting God's plan for His own glory through the centuries. The Bible itself reveals the history of God's love and grace for mankind from creation to the end of time. Because our big *why* of homeschooling, our purpose for teaching our children and teens, consists of loving God and loving others, studying how God has demonstrated love toward mankind and how mankind has responded to Him and to one another . . . that's the heart of our efforts, right there.

Centering on Bible and History

I emphasized that knowing your *why* for homeschooling makes everything else easier – it shows you what to focus on and helps you know what is unimportant. If you go back to your own family's *why* you will likely find a subject or two that jumps out at you. This is your own foundational subject, the emphasis that will shape everything else you teach. Trust me, that makes things so much easier!

How does this work? Take a look at how our central courses of Bible and history frame our homeschool each year, each semester, every week. Rain or shine, sickness and health, good times and undercaffeinated zombie days, we can have success by staying true to our focus.

Bible

Each day begins with "Bible time," a reading from a Bible storybook like *Illustrated Family Bible Stories* or study from a family devotional like *A Family Guide to Narnia,* or just a few verses of Scripture with discussion and prayer. Each student memorizes Bible verses and learns study skills in AWANA. On weeks we don't have AWANA work, we memorize other verses together.

We take our Bible studies deeper with personal application. I might spend a couple weeks talking about how to take notes in church, how to use Bible study tools, and how to share the gospel with a friend. We read missionary biographies (what boy is not inspired by David Livingston?). High schoolers take a Bible overview course for at least one year, a semester each of Old Testament and New Testament survey with these books. (I prefer to have them complete those the year they study ancient history.)

How do we help our student study Bible independently?

Since Bible is a foundational subject, I remain more hands-on with Bible than with other subjects. We do read together each morning and frequently discuss Scriptural truths we are learning together. Yet students need to learn skills for independent study:

I encourage my teen to have regular private devotions. I do not require them to show me or prove their private time. Their personal relationship with God is as personal and private as mine is, and I do not expect them to read my own devotional journal. I do provide materials to help him get started, like a study Bible, devotional, or journal.

I require my teen to complete a year of AWANA work for school credit.

I also require my teen to complete the Bible overview study and/or church history written work included in my history curriculum on paper and file it away, not for grades but for proof of completion. I ask my teen to let me glance over it every couple of weeks.

How do I show proof of work?

For Bible, we save the AWANA book (signed by their AWANA leader) and a binder of Bible study notes and church history research. I throw all of these into the Rubbermaid container at the end of the year. This is the only subject in which simple completion earns an A.

Bible is not a requirement for graduation. But if the student completes one AWANA book and a couple hours a week of study in church history, missionary biographies, Bible overview, and/or worldview along with some written work to demonstrate knowledge gained, I will give the student one credit of Bible on his transcript. This fulfills an elective credit.

History

Since history is, alongside Bible, foundational to our family's homeschool *why*, nary a homeschool week goes by that we have not studied this subject. If we are sick, we are reading history books in bed and watching history videos. If we are busy and overwhelmed, we are discussing history in the minivan. If we are on vacation, we are visiting museums, historical sites, and cultural events.

There is simply no such thing as "being behind in history" in our house. Just not gonna' happen. History is who we are.

Now, if you are a classical or Charlotte Mason homeschooler, this may be true of you, too. Homeschoolers who organize their learning on a four-year cycle of world studies find themselves centering their literature, writing, research, and art projects around their history studies. Yet still the homeschool *why* takes this a step deeper.

If your history studies (or science, or English, or whatever you chose to support your *why*) are central to communicating your family's purpose, vision, ministry, and relationships, this once burdensome subject is

92

suddenly light with meaning. It is *who you are,* not just something you do. It is *how you relate to God and mankind,* not just answers on a paper. It is *a relationship with your child,* not just a stack of books to get through somehow.

So how does that work in the daily grind of homeschooling? In our homeschool, I plan our entire school year around what we are studying in history. That curriculum (in our case, Tapestry of Grace, but there are many similar curricula) forms the basis for our school calendar, our semester dates, our weekly emphasis. At the beginning of the school year, I plan when each semester and quarter of our history course will begin and end, and even put these dates on the family calendar. Now the whole family is on the same page.

Each week, I make our lesson plans two weeks ahead of time for history. I may not plan far ahead in any other subject, but I know where we are going and what we are doing in history -- because that affects everything about our week. When I see exciting new topics coming up in the next few weeks, I alert my husband and children so they know where we are going: World War 2 next month, or three weeks on South America starting soon, or ancient Egypt in two weeks. We all start looking forward to the topic, planning for things we want to do in conjunction with our studies, and working together to get the most out of each lesson.

When I am making the lesson plans, I also log into our public library catalog and place holds for materials. I look for books, videos, and reference materials that will make our studies come alive.

On Mondays, I give out the week's assignments and my high schooler plans her week of work. At the top of every assignment notebook for elementary and middle school students, I write the history reading for that week because that subject is the cornerstone for the other academic pursuits.

Then the rest of our studies in the humanities coincide with our history for that week. We study literature, geography, government, church history, comparative religion, philosophy, worldview, art history, and music history from the perspective of what our history lesson covers that week. Now, we cannot possibly touch on every one of those subjects every week, but we can usually pull information and resources on several of them.

For instance, when learning about British colonialism and trade in India, we studied the geography and history of that subcontinent. We learned about the beginnings of Buddhism and Hinduism, and we visited an Asian art museum for a private tour with a docent who showed the children how to find common elements in Indian art of this period. Then we read about the missionary Adoniram Judson who ministered in nearby Burma during this period.

That seems all very involved, but it only took two additional hours of reading aloud in addition to our regular history reading and then one afternoon's field trip; all of this spread over the course of a week or two. We each gained valuable insights into this period of history, the beliefs of others, and how these influenced their actions.

How do I help my student study independently?

Again, since history is a core subject for us, I am more hands-on with this subject than with others. Yet still my teen completes the majority of the work on his own time:

- I give my teen a list of required reading at the beginning of the week. He does that as well as any independent research necessary to grasp the lesson before discussion time.

- Comprehension questions are included in the curriculum. Whether or not the student uses them just to study or writes down the answers is up to him so long as he thoroughly understands the lesson.

How do I hold the student accountable?

This is such an important course for me that I hold students doubly accountable for each lesson:

- Each week, we hold a deep history discussion for all the students together for over two hours.

- We cover not only what happened and with whom, but also the resultant worldview issues that are raised. This discussion also pulls in geography, government, church history, and philosophical concepts. I expect the students to come prepared with fresh insights and thoughtful questions based on that week's reading and research.

- Every Friday, the high school student completes a written test that includes short answer questions and one long essay on that week's lesson.

- Once a quarter, the student completes a comprehensive cumulative written exam that includes all the history, geography, and government for the year so far. It takes over an hour and includes maps, timelines, short answers, definitions, a short essay, and one or two longer essays.

History is my one hard course. I am confident that if my students survive history at home, they will not only know how to think and live in the world they encounter, but they also can survive nearly any academic course they will ever take! Ha!

What if your family's emphasis is not on the subject matter God gifted your individual student?

My oldest son always knew he would study the sciences when he grew up. He told me when he was ten he would be a scientist, and he narrowed his focus to mathematics as a senior. I gave him plenty of opportunities to study science and math at his own pace. Yet we still kept Bible and history at the forefront.

Why? *Because of our family's homeschool why.* No matter what path God has for each of my children, no matter the careers, and ministries they each fulfill, they still have the same two most important duties: *love God and love others.* And even *work hard at both.* My husband and I knew that saturating them with the truths of God's Word and the records of

His dealing with mankind was the best possible preparation for those duties.

Now in college, my son has found his Bachelor of Science program includes no history or geography and little literature. I am relieved to know that he has a firm grasp of – and a healthy appreciation for – how God has worked over time.

In my state of Texas, students are required to earn three credits in social studies (one American history, one-half each in government and economics, one in world history or geography). You may check your own state's requirements by googling your state name and then "high school graduation requirements" or by checking the HSLDA recommendations. Because of our heavy emphasis, extensive research, and heavy project assignments, I give each teen a credit for *honors history* each year of high school. This is one of the few courses I can confidently give honors credit in, and I will share how I determine that when we cover transcripts in chapter 20.

Choose the foundational subject right for your homeschool.

Bible and history form the basis of our family's homeschool. My husband and I feel confident that by emphasizing Bible and history in our homeschool, we will fulfill our own homeschool *why* and succeed in our highest parenting goal: demonstrating our love for God and love for others by working hard at what He has given us to do. Take a look at your own homeschool priorities and mission, then find the core learning that is right for your family. Homeschooling is a relationship with your child, not just a stack of books to get through somehow.

9. English

A word fitly spoken is like apples of gold in a setting of silver.

Like a gold ring or an ornament of gold is a wise reprover to a listening ear.

Like the cold of snow in the time of harvest is a faithful messenger to those who send him; he refreshes the soul of his masters.

-- Proverbs 25:11-13

IN THE LAST CHAPTER, I shared with you the central focus of our family's homeschool: Bible and history. And I talked about how you can identify your own homeschool's most important subjects by examining your own homeschool *why*.

Nevertheless, we must cover more than one or two classes in high school, right? So now I tackle what is likely the second most important subject after your own core subject – **English.**

In this broad category of high school study, we find grammar, writing, literature, vocabulary, spelling, and speech. A lot of ground to cover for just one credit a year, isn't it? How can we stay sane while making sure our student has what he needs to succeed? Can one homeschool mom possibly cover all that material adequately without making it a full-time job?

Absolutely, we can. I know from experience that teens *can* be taught to write, they *can* be taught to read and analyze classic literature, they *can* be trained to broaden their vocabulary, and they *can* be trained to communicate effectively. We don't have to make this our life's main focus to ensure this happens, either. Even English can be made easy!

"That's fine for you to say, Lea Ann," you are likely thinking. "You are an author yourself, so you probably love teaching writing. Your children no doubt have your writing abilities. I'm too artsy/sciency/crafty to be an effective writing or literature teacher." People tell me that a lot, and it makes me laugh. Because you know what? *I didn't realize I could write well until I started teaching writing to my teens.*

It was actually during our years working with the *WriteShop* program that I understood that some of my instincts – and a lot of my mother's homeschooling – were actually part of a logic that makes writing work. I spent those middle school years and early high school years fine-tuning that system which makes writing simple for essays and academic writing. So well before he graduated from high school, my science-minded mathematician could confidently turn in a writing assignment on any subject. He knew the steps to follow to succeed, and he has the confidence to apply in any situation: research papers, paragraphs, essay tests, college essays, and now college papers. Now he is successfully applying those same strategies to his college papers.

Since then, I have discovered *Jenson's Format Writing*. Using this straightforward, no-nonsense workbook with my middle school son, we are honing in on basic skills that make paragraphs, essays, and research papers easy (or at least *easier*) to write. We both see a tremendous difference every week.

So how do we pass on the keys to English success to our students? How do we ensure our high schoolers have what it takes both to communicate effectively as adults and to evaluate what they are seeing, hearing, and reading in the world? **We simply build on their language arts foundation systematically for the entirety of the high school years.**

I am going to lay out this foundation in pretty broad, general terms and allow *you* to customize it to fit your student best. You know where your own student's strengths and weaknesses lie, and you know your own student's individual talents and interests best. Here is a sample plan to tackle four years of English study at the high school level.

Remember, your graduation requirements will likely include three or four years of English. I would strongly recommend every student complete English language arts studies for the entire four years and that at least one semester each year focus on writing. **This one academic subject directly influences success in every future academic and career pursuit.** "People do judge you by the words you use," as an advertisement frequently reminded me throughout my childhood. Every hour spent on writing is an investment in the student's future.

High School English Made Easy

Your goal before graduation is to train your student so he can . . .

- read and comprehend what he read, whether it's a textbook, novel, instruction manual, or persuasive essay,
- communicate effectively his understanding of what he read or heard,
- produce paragraphs and essays that demonstrate both his knowledge of a subject *and* his command of the English language, and
- recognize errors in sentence structure, grammar, and punctuation and remedy those mistakes himself.

If he can do all four of the above, your student will score well on college entrance exams, produce an effective college essay, impress his first employer, and meet the challenges of his first college courses. You can help him achieve those goals.

Ok, here is a general guideline or benchmark to make the most of these high school English credits. Feel free to tailor these suggestions to your own child's needs and interests. If your student has already mastered the early steps in middle school, then move on to what the student needs next. A student could be working on more than one of these areas at once (for instance, my students usually take English grammar and literature concurrently). Regardless of the specific curriculum and goals used, *students must be reading quality literature the entire four years*. Students cannot recognize proper grammar and produce creative writing of their own if they are not regularly reading.

1. Write a complete sentence (expressing a complete thought) with proper capitalization and punctuation. The student will recognize fragment and run-on sentences and fix those errors. A student can also identify the parts of

speech and either label or diagram them. [course: English grammar]

2. Write a strong paragraph including a topic sentence, several supporting sentences, and a concluding sentence. The student will use complete sentences of varying structure and complexity while still using proper capitalization and punctuation. The student can identify being verbs and rewrite the sentence using action verbs. [course: English writing]

3. Read classic literature of various genres: poetry, biographies, historical fiction, literary fiction, humor, romance, etc. [course: literature or other assigned reading]

4. Write longer essays and papers involving research, persuasion, documentation, and multiple drafts over a period of weeks. [course: English writing, history, literature, or other courses that require reports]

5. Analyze literature, identifying themes, characterization, motifs, and literary devices in

classic works, comparing and contrasting with other writings. [course: English literature]

If you view high school English as a spiral that continues from the student's middle school years through graduation, you can see how new skills are added while the main idea – writing – builds into all of it. Just like in elementary school, your high school student must be reading and writing every week of every year. You are just going to kick it up a notch each semester, adding the skill or reinforcing the weakness that your student faces.

Simply build on the student's language arts foundation systematically for the entirety of the high school years.

How does this look for an average student? Here's what happened with my oldest son, the science-minded mathematician with very average English skills and no desire to ever pick up a book or a pencil. By the end of middle school, he had already completed a year of grammar and composition and one year of *WriteShop I* (how to write a good paragraph).

- **Freshman year:** He complained that he couldn't remember the parts of speech well, so we took grammar and composition for his main text. He read 19th-century literature including *Pride and Prejudice, Les Miserables, Great Expectations, The Scarlet Letter,* and *Crime and Punishment* as well as shorter works by authors like Twain, Melville, and Goethe.

- **Sophomore year:** He was ready for more writing after a year of heavy grammar, so we returned to *WriteShop 2*. He also enrolled in the online literature class this year, where he learned to analyze 20th-century works like *All Quiet on the Western Front, Animal Farm,* and *Lord of the Flies,* along with many others. Besides his weekly writing assignments with me, he gave quarterly oral presentations to his class.

- **Junior year:** His writing was solid, his understanding of grammar clear, and his appreciation for literature growing. I enrolled him in another year of online literature, where he tackled ancient literature. I gave him writing assignments weekly or bi-weekly, most of them based on his work in other subjects, especially history and worldview.

- **Senior year:** At this point, he had completed all his English requirements for graduation. He led literature discussion with his younger sister, teaching her the concepts and techniques he had learned in the past two years. He wrote essays at least once a week on a topic related to literature, Bible, history, or worldview.

The result? Even though my science-minded son would still claim to hate reading and writing, his college placement tests put him in the highest level of freshman English in college, and he found his writing class the easiest of his first semester courses.

Did you see my strategy? I found what he needed each year (a little more writing, or help with grammar) and planned his curriculum around that. By his last two years, he was simply practicing what he already knew, developing habits that would contribute to his future academic pursuits.

Here is the point I am making about English: give your student what he needs and continue tailoring his training to his abilities. Do not get trapped into merely handing him the next workbook or signing up for the next class. Look at your student, find what he needs next, and focus on that. English will be easier for him if it is just at his own level.

How do I help my student study independently?

When we think about writing class, we think about hours and hours and pages and pages. That is not what writing class looks like in our house, though. Here is how we make it easy:

- If my student is studying grammar, I use an easy-to-follow workbook. My student is responsible for completing half of the book and the corresponding tests before Christmas, and he must complete the entire course by June. He grades his own homework once a week. I will answer any questions, but so far my high schoolers are doing great on their own.

- Students must read good literature weekly, in addition to our family read-aloud.

- Once the student has learned the steps to writing, I do not micromanage those, either. When the student is first learning how to write, I will require my student to turn in brainstorming sheets, rough drafts, and edits at intervals. When the student becomes more confident, the student may complete all the stages independently, then staple them all together and turn them in at one time. Then once the student has mastered the process, he can just turn in the final copy by the due date. I give clear due dates and consequences for not turning the assignment in on time. The student can decide how to pace the assignment at that point.

How do I hold the student accountable?

English has straightforward accountability built into the subject.

- For grammar and vocabulary, I proctor tests. Vocabulary tests come weekly. My student can decide when to take grammar tests my oldest would do a whole stack of tests at one time, but my daughter preferred to complete about one a week). I do proctor and grade the tests.

- Literature is a discussion class. If the student takes an online literature class, he receives a discussion grade, and the course we use requires quite detailed answers to earn an A.

- I use rubrics to grade essays so my students understand how to improve next time. The rubric helps me stay consistent with my grading, as well. Many writing courses provide sample grading rubrics, or you can find them online.

10. Math

Do not worry about your difficulties in Mathematics.
I can assure you mine are still greater.
--Albert Einstein

WHILE WE LOOK at individual subjects our homeschool high school students face, let's keep remembering our two most important principles:

Your *why* will make each course, every decision, every class easier. Keep your priorities in focus to maintain clarity.

Your student learns best *his way*, using his own learning style and his own pace.

There is no subject this is more apparent than mathematics. Your student will complete three or four years of math in high school (depending on your state's requirements). The exact subjects he studies will depend on what level he begins in high school. This, in turn, depends on two things:

- how much math he completed middle school, and

- how quickly his brain matures to handle algebra.

I want to talk about that last point a bit because this is something *I really wish someone had explained to me when my first student was in middle school.* This is the one fact that would have saved my teen and me over a year of frustration, agony, disagreement, and despair. It would have saved us both from hours of raised voices and crumpled papers, blaming and scribbling. Because once we both understood this fact, our math lives were never the same. I'm giving you the secret, and you're going to write it down and memorize it and apply it and watch the clouds part over your math lessons, too. Ready? Here goes:

Until your student achieves the mental maturity for abstract thinking, algebra is a big waste of time at best and roadblock to academic pursuit at worst.

It does not matter how fast your child learns math facts. It does not matter how quickly he races through math workbooks in elementary. It does not matter how much he loves using math in middle school. It does not matter how bright he is, how articulate he is, how quick he is with his figures. **He will not comprehend algebra until his brain grows into it.**

You cannot rush mental maturity. You cannot force it, you cannot push it along, you cannot lesson plan it. Like physical growth and puberty, each student will reach mental milestones *at his own pace,* according to a God-ordained timetable that we cannot see. We can expect this maturity to occur within a general time frame, and we can even guess based on external physical clues, but we just don't know for certain when that mental growth spurt is going to occur.

That is why I firmly believe parents should avoid algebra until the student demonstrates maturity in abstract thinking. In my experience, the student will, at that point, take off at a rapid pace and complete his math requirements with far less effort than if we force the subject before he is ready.

Sometime between ages 14 and 16 (sometimes younger for girls), students experience this mental growth. Up until this point, their learning is very literal. They learn words for what they experience with their own senses. They apply rules for what happens in their own lives. They learn from their five senses, using skills of visual, auditory, and kinesthetic learning. Therefore, this is how they learn math: by manipulating objects, describing the patterns they experience in nature and time, and memorizing math facts that they know by experience hold true in their real world.

Algebra changes everything. Suddenly, students must imagine a world in which nothing is literal, letters represent abstract concepts, and patterns occur on imaginary horizontal and vertical planes. *None of this makes sense in their universe.* Students try with varying success to apply this to the literal world they live in, but soon the lessons and concepts become so abstract and complicated that application to money or counting objects or cups of water becomes seemingly impossible. Math has become to the student, at this point, entirely abstract.

There are two possible choices for a student at this point. In my case, as a thirteen-year-old homeschool student, I chose **the faith route**. I decided math was an abstract game that meant absolutely nothing to my real-world existence, so I would just play the game to win. I copied down the rules my textbook told me to follow. I memorized formulas that meant absolutely nothing to me. Then I taught myself that when the question uses certain words, use this formula; if it says other words, use the other formula. I played this game successfully for four years, completing two years of algebra, trigonometry, calculus, physics, and college statistics successfully by blindly following these rules. I never understood a thing I was doing.

When my oldest son turned the corner from pre-algebra to algebra around the same age, he refused to take abstract math on faith. He insisted on choosing **the fight to understand**. When he missed a problem, I

119

would point to the formula with vigor. *Do it this way!*
That response was not good enough for
him. "*Why?* Why does it work? Why is that the rule?
What does the answer mean? How does this apply to
the real world?"

"I do not care! Do it.this way to get an A!" That
answer infuriated him. Voices raised. Pencils flew. He
had to see the answer, and he wanted it to be as clear as
understanding why six groups of seven are forty-two
and why two halves equal three-sixths. He had to know
it, to see it clearly in his mind, even while I insisted it
did not matter, that he just had to have faith and get it
right. I insisted on the faith route, but he was fighting
for real understanding.

His progress in Algebra 1 faltered. He poured
over his textbook. He muttered under his breath. He
ignored my pleas just to memorize the formula.

Suddenly, one day, he got it. I remember the
morning he ran down the stairs. "I see it! It all makes
sense!" Every day of high school math after that, he did
not work a minute. He knew the answer without trying.
He even tried in vain to explain calculus to me

(something about undulating waves with spiraling triangles that look different from different angles . . . I still do not know).

I have asked him so many times what made the difference. He insists that he just woke up and understood. In that moment, everything his book said made sense, and he could see the figures and lines and shapes moving in his mind, and he knew what the formulas and problems and abstract equations all meant. From that moment, he loved the subject, tutoring his friends in algebra and trigonometry and even choosing a math major in college.

When he describes a sine wave or why a formula works or how shapes change in space, he actually giggles. He giggles like his sister does when she finds a new flavor of lip gloss. It is so funny, but obviously, math has become a source of joy for him.

There is a moral to this story:

Each student will reach mental milestones at his own pace, according to a God-ordained timetable that we cannot see.

If I had it all to do over again, if I knew then what I know now, I would have held off Algebra 1 another six months or a year. Those arguments, frustrations, and crumpled papers were a complete waste of time. He could have better spent his time studying another year of prealgebra, consumer math, or more arithmetic. Once his brain grew into it, his high school math was a piece of cake. In fact, in fewer than four years he completed plenty of math:

- Algebra 1
- Algebra 2
- Geometry
- Trigonometry
- Pre-Calculus

He tested out of the first year of college calculus without studying for the test. By that point, higher math just *made sense.*

The key to successful high school math is staying sensitive to your own student's maturity. My teen daughter was obviously ready for algebra quickly. She went seamlessly from prealgebra in seventh grade to algebra in eighth grade with no problems at all. Her high school math journey will look something like this:

- Geometry
- Algebra 2
- Trigonometry
- Pre-calculus

I do not anticipate her needing more than that; she is not planning to pursue the sciences, so she will complete more than enough math for high school graduation and college acceptance.

My middle school student is *not* ready for algebra yet, though he also completed prealgebra in seventh grade. I noticed he tripped over the beginning abstract concepts and struggled with some of the geometry. He could do it, but it was excruciating mental work, not obvious facts to him. Recognizing he had not reached that mental leap to abstract thinking, I gave him a review of prealgebra and introduction to abstract reasoning in eighth grade using a different curriculum.

I have found a great resource to bridge that gap is *Principles of Mathematics* (MasterBooks). This is a two-year prealgebra course, and my eighth grader completed both of them in one year for review. The author carefully explains the reasoning behind formulas and algebraic actions and applies them to real-life scenarios. The equations and lessons build in complexity while remaining practical, so students get that mental workout necessary for algebra later. This course provides a bridge between practical and abstract mathematics for young teens not yet ready for algebra.

During that eighth grade year, I could see mental changes as my son approached his fourteenth birthday. He is ready to begin algebra at his own pace. His high school math will likely look like this:

- Algebra 1
- Geometry
- Algebra 2
- Trigonometry

If he were to pursue the sciences *or even a degree in mathematics,* that course still provides enough high school math. I learned from the head of mathematics at Liberty University (the largest Christian liberal arts college in the world) that high school calculus is not expected, even for math majors. In fact, most science and engineering students have little or no exposure to calculus before high school graduation. Instead, a working knowledge of geometry and a solid algebra foundation are far more important for college success.

Are we cheating our students if we do not push higher math?

Absolutely not. I have actually asked math educators in public and private schools this exact question. I specifically asked why Chinese students are doing so much better than American students when we know the mental maturity cannot be externally controlled. Both the Asian educators I asked gave me the same answer. The difference between the high-performing Chinese students and our American low-scoring ones is not how early they learn algebra. The big missing ingredient is both *application and comprehension.*

The Chinese push for *mastery* in math, so students learn rote facts and formulas, much more like my own faith-based approach to higher math. In the end, they score great on tests but struggle to apply their education to real-world problems. They may take calculus in 9th grade but, like me, they will have no idea what they are doing on paper. American students in institutional education may be pushed along with a crowd of students ahead of their ability or even behind their capability, so each individual student may not achieve the level of learning, understanding, and application they are fully capable of. We do not want to follow either example.

Homeschool students have a unique advantage in math education. We can wait for our teen to grow into maturity and then allow him to take off at his own pace, achieving mastery at his own personal best. That, my friend, is when our homeschool *why* makes the very most of a math education.

Homeschool High School Math Made Easy

Your goal before graduation is to prepare your student for college and life:

- use math consumer math responsibly in his banking account, purchasing, and employment, and understand how math works in loans, taxes, and economics,

- successfully complete algebra, geometry, and perhaps other advanced math courses at his own pace,
- apply his math education and reasoning to other subjects, and
- assist others around him in math understanding and application.

How do I help my student study independently?

Your student will be successful at learning math on his own if he is at his own appropriate level and pace. First, make sure your student can handle the material you have given, and then keep him moving forward as he is able. He may sprint through the easy parts, and then slow down on difficult concepts. As long as he is working and making progress over time, he will do well.

How do I hold the student accountable?

This is so easy: grade his tests. Math is right or wrong, and students demonstrate their logic on paper or they do not. Math is one subject that is cut and dry.

- By Algebra 1, I no longer grade homework. My student can check his own work each day to make sure he is working the problems correctly. Getting instant feedback on whether or not he is doing it right really helps reinforce learning.

- I do not even care if the student does all the homework. Usually, they do not finish every review problem on every lesson once they hit their stride in math; they just glance over what the upcoming test is over and practice a few hard problems. If this works and the grades are good, I do not micromanage the homework.

- The test is closed book using only graph paper and a calculator. The student should show his work so I can judge if he applied the correct formula and logic to each problem. These tests make up the entire subject's grade.

128

High school math really can be easy if we allow each student to learn at his own pace. It really makes all the difference.

11. Science

Science without religion is lame, religion without
science is blind.
-- Albert Einstein

WE CONTINUE OUR OVERVIEW of homeschool high school subjects with the one that is perhaps the most dreaded of all: **Science.** Science is hard and science is messy, but science is required so we cannot get around it.

Science is also essential. The scientific advances of the past century continue to propel our world forward, changing every part of our lives from birth to communication to transportation to recreation. The science classes I endured as a homeschool teen over two decades ago contained a wealth of information that neither I nor my parents could anticipate would be so important, like computer programming and bioethics. Before I had the opportunity to begin teaching the same to my own teens, science's seemingly dry facts and diagrams had become the basis of ethical, political, and societal dilemmas we all face every day:

- nutrition, diet, and food safety
- health, wellness, and vaccinations
- reproduction, reproductive rights, and family planning
- controlled substances, legalized drugs, and chemical and biological warfare,
- ecology, recycling, and environmental activism
- satellite communication, space travel, and the search for life on other planets

That is just the tip of the iceberg. My science textbooks barely discussed most of the above issues and definitely not to the extent they are debated today. What further scientific knowledge will fuel the worldview issues of our teen's generation?

We cannot know it all. For most of us who are not scientists, we cannot even comprehend most of these subjects. It behooves us, however, to prepare our teens for the coming questions they will face.

Our goal for high school science is not merely to pass the required courses for graduation, to fulfill the arbitrary lab requirements, and to check off the worksheet questions. Our aim is to provide our students with the knowledge to *comprehend* the basis of modern scientific study and to *discern* the inherent moral and spiritual values.

This is why **science gets to the heart of your homeschool *why*.** Take a deep breath and look back at your homeschool *why* statement. Then make sure you are fully prepared to prioritize those important goals in your science studies.

Overall, your goal before graduation is to prepare your student in these areas:

- Fulfill your state's graduation requirements for high school science. For many teens, that means two or three years of lab-based biology, chemistry, and physics or other elective science courses.

- Read and comprehend scientific articles, graphs, tables, and experiment reports.

- Understand the scientific method, apply it to his own experiments, and document any findings.

- Learn the foundational concepts of each branch of science studied and memorize the key scientific laws, formulas, and models that shape current thought.

- Recognize the differing worldviews in the scientific community, particularly the difference between humanistic evolution and biblical Christianity, and understand how these views affect research and interpretation data.

- Evaluate ethical disagreements in society and discern if scientific findings correctly or irresponsibly support the position.

This is a lot of work, but remember that we have four entire years to touch on all of it. Keeping in mind your *why* will really help you and your teen soldier through it all.

Here are some additional tips to keep science simple:

- The courses that *must* be completed for **graduation** should be finished first. This ensures everything is accomplished and also prepares the student for the upcoming college entrance exams.

- The student should practice reading and answering questions on science articles, graphs, etc., as well as applying the scientific method to prepare **college entrance exams.** Familiarity with foundational concepts of biology, chemistry, and physics will make this portion of the test much easier to complete.

- Analyze worldview presuppositions and discuss ethical dilemmas to prepare the student for **real-life** problems he will face as an adult.

Science easily overwhelms me. However, when I keep these above principles in mind, the subject becomes much easier.

How do I fulfill the science requirements?

Wondering what to study? Here are some ways to fulfill the graduation requirements.

When I was a homeschool student back in the dark ages, I fulfilled my science requirements with these courses:

- high school biology (with lab)
- high school chemistry (with lab and microscope! That was a big deal back then)
- high school physics
- computer (one semester. I thought it was a waste of time, but my father thought maybe computers might become a big deal some day, even though we were the only family I knew who owned one. I learned binary code which *was* a waste of time.)

When my oldest son graduated, he had completed the following courses:

- physical science (with lab)
- biology (with lab)
- chemistry (with lab)
- physics (with lab)

My high school daughter is not as interested in science. In her second year of high school, she decided she preferred to focus on the humanities. Our state requires three years of science for graduation, but she prioritized her most difficult subjects first. Her transcript will include the following:

- biology (with lab)
- chemistry (with lab)
- anatomy
- an elective or even no science her senior year

How do I help my student study independently?

When we think about science class, we think about labs and chemicals and lectures. This may be the case if your student takes science in a co-op class or online tutorial. Science in your homeschool, though, may be much different. Here is how you can make science easy:

- Use a high quality, student-friendly textbook. My favorites right now are the Master Books science courses for this reason.
- Attend conferences and lectures on biblical creationism to enhance your student's understanding. We try to catch events by the Institute for Creation Research whenever possible.
- Visit science museums, fairs, and other events in your area, and discuss the exhibits and value statements together.
- Encourage your student to ask thoughtful questions of the scientists in his life: doctors, chemists, engineers, and educators.

How do I hold the student accountable?

Your science curriculum likely has straightforward accountability built into it.

- Give your student closed-book tests regularly.

- Require lab notebooks for laboratory courses, and show your student how to properly document his work. (If he applies to an exclusive college for a science major, he may need to produce this notebook as proof of work).

- Teach your student how to write a research paper (English!), and then require one or two formal reports a year in each course.

High school science can seem overwhelming for the homeschool parent and student. Nevertheless, by keeping the homeschool *why* in focus and prioritizing the subject goals, these courses can become some of the most practical the student learns.

12. Electives

Leadership and learning are indispensable to each other. John F. Kennedy

We have looked at how typical homeschool teens will fulfill requirements in Bible, history, English, math, and science. These subjects make up the bulk of your student's transcript and prepare your student for college entrance exams and applications.

However, these are not enough. Four or five classes do not a year of high school make, and your state's graduation requirement will likely include a few more courses. Never fear, intrepid homeschool mom. If you can brave those core subjects we already discussed, the rest is easy. I promise.

Not convinced? I will prove it. By now you should have googled your state's graduation requirements. If your teen has a favorite college or two, you may have even looked up admissions requirements (don't panic if you haven't; it's not a must . . . yet). Take a look now at what additional classes you can consider. Your list may include the following:

- speech
- foreign language
- physical education
- fine arts
- sports
- other electives

How can we make sure our teens complete these requirements while remaining true to our homeschool *why* and keeping things as simple as possible? I'll tell you how: give your teen choices.

I mentioned in chapter 3 that the first year or two, students would do well to concentrate on their main subjects and requirements for high school. As much as possible, we save electives until the senior year. This is for three important reasons:

1. Students usually take their college entrance exams (ACT or SAT) during their junior year of high school. These tests cover the basic material high school students learn in English, math, and science for all four years. *The best test preparation is a solid education.*

2. Your student may begin contacting colleges as early as his junior year. When discussing admissions requirements and scholarship opportunities, he will be grateful his transcript shows that he has already completed most of the university's requirements for admissions (surprisingly, college admissions requirements may be considerably lower than his state's graduation requirements).

3. After the push toward college and career his junior year, both student and mom may be academically exhausted and less than motivated for that final year. It will be a welcome relief to enjoy fun classes with less strenuous

requirements in the end, if not a significantly lighter workload.

For all of those reasons, I highly recommend homeschool high school students take *over* their minimum credits each year. For the first three years, students should take every required subject and perhaps an elective or two. Not sure what I mean by that? That's because this is a math problem:

- Find the minimum number of credits required to graduate in your state (in Texas, that's 22). Divide that number by 4 and round up. This is the minimum number of classes your student needs for the first few years of high school (in Texas, that means at least 6 credits, but I prefer 7).

- Look at specific subjects your state requires for more than one year (in Texas, that includes English, Math, Science, Social Studies/History, and Foreign Language). Require your student to take those classes every year he completes the requirements.

144

- Fill in that year's remaining credits with single-year credits required (in Texas, that's one credit of Fine Arts, one credit of PE, and 5 credits other electives).

When you do this exercise, you will likely find that your student has no choices for freshman and sophomore years; the academic plan is clear. Nevertheless, this exercise also quite hopeful -- when chemistry gets tough or foreign language becomes boring, the student can count down the days until the class done, and he will never have to do it again. Hooray!

For the first two years of high school, our students take 7-8 credits. That means they meet the minimum graduation requirements in our state by the end of the junior year, at which point they technically could graduate (but they do not because they are not ready in other ways). The senior year, my students work hard to bring up their GPA for scholarships and relax into easier classes while working full time and saving up for college.

So in our homeschool, a typical high school program for the freshman or sophomore year looks like this:

- English
- Math (the required Algebra 1 or Geometry)
- Science (from the required biology or chemistry with labs)
- Social Studies/History
- Foreign Language (Spanish because of our family background)
- Bible (considered an elective in our state)
- Fine Arts (private music lessons and either choir or orchestra along with music history and art appreciation, also an elective)
- PE (competitive soccer and/or referee certification)

In the junior and senior years, students can drop subjects after they have met the minimum requirements. However, I will require our most important foundational subjects all four years since that is the heart of our homeschooling. So in our homeschool, teens take Bible and world history all four years whether they like it or not. Fine arts is a required course until age 18 because my husband said so, and he's the boss. Ha!

By his senior year, my oldest did not have empty elective requirements he had to fulfill. Because he had studied Bible and fine arts every year and PE three years, as well as an extra two years of math credit, he had accumulated more credits than he needed to graduate with a distinguished program of study (honors level). My teen daughter will likely find herself in the same situation.

In the likely event your student is *not* using up all his credits with PE and music like we do, here are some more ideas for extra elective credits:

- Take 4 years of subjects only required for 3 years (extra science, math, or history).
- Double up on a favorite subject in the senior year (take physics AND anatomy).
- Take more foreign language (our students take 4 years instead of the required 2).

- Add worldview, church history, computers, or other interests.

How do I help my student study independently?

Just as in the core courses, be sure to document these electives and objectively grade them. Help your student find a curriculum or program that will enable him to study on his own using his own learning strengths, yet enables him to prove his knowledge in an objective way with tests, computer print-outs, projects, or certifications.

How do I hold the student accountable?

Find the objective measurement for success according to the curriculum or program the student chose. It may be a grade average on the computer software course, a certification in a skill, or completion of a project or test. Then give deadlines. Hold the student accountable for completing each course (or half of a course) by the end of each semester. This is important preparation for future college work and life in general.

13. Growing Into Adulthood: Changing Family Relationships

I T IS TIME TO TAKE A STEP back from the academics of the high school years. As important as those classes are, as stressful as planning the courses may be, and as hard as we are working to make it all easy on the family, there's still something much more critical to keep in mind: **this teen is quickly turning into an adult.**

No matter what our homeschool why may be, that primary purpose has something to do with that *end result*. We are not homeschooling to keep them little (don't we wish!). We are not homeschooling because preteens smell like roses (obviously!). We are not homeschooling because every mother wishes she were joined at the hip to her teen son (*big sigh*). No, **we**

are homeschooling because of the adults we pray our students will become.

So when we approach the high school years, we arrive at a life stage that suddenly *does* beg the socialization question. Adulthood largely occurs *outside* the home, in the big, scary world beyond our front yard, among crowds of strangers of various backgrounds, beliefs, and demographics. So while, during elementary, we may have taken the time to *shelter* somewhat, and during the middle school years we may have begun *training* how to handle new situations, during high school life skills takes on a new purpose. Kids, it is time to start adulting.

We can—and should—take this preparation seriously. We have four years to build responsibility, work ethic, discernment, wisdom, and social skills into our young people. Whether they go to college or straight to career, whether they stay home or move across the country, whether they work a secular job or serve in full-time ministry, *our young people must be prepared to take personal responsibility for their lives.*

It would be completely unfair and unrealistic to treat our teens as children for their entire adolescence and then suddenly at age eighteen expect mature behavior, choices, and responsibility. Similarly, it is unhealthy and unloving for homeschool parents to stand in the way of our young adults stepping forth into the future God created them to realize. Our task as homeschool parents of teens is to smooth that transition for our young people as much as possible, to offer them training and practice so they can gradually begin managing their own choices, responsibilities, and outcomes.

That feels a little heavy sometimes. The thought of your thirteen or fifteen-year-old student living away from home and paying bills and making life choices can make a mother ill. For crying out loud, imagining my eighteen-year-old on his own and in charge of his decisions renders me lightheaded at times. I may have been hitting the essential oils pretty hard.

The truth is, though, that this new life stage need not be utterly terrifying. Whenever my husband and I begin to fret (because parenting teens and young adults give you *plenty of opportunities* to fret!), we remind ourselves of these two principles:

1. We did give our teen ample opportunity to begin practicing these adult responsibilities during high school.
2. We did learn *a lot* from our own mistakes in our twenties.

The older our children become, the less control we parents exert.

When they were babies, we could literally schedule their entire days. When they were toddlers, we could even schedule their bathroom habits. As they grew into elementary, we chose their friends, their outfits, and their entertainment. However, as they grew through puberty and into the teen years, our young people began asserting their own personality, preferences, and even choices.

In the high school years, this natural feeling of autonomy continues to grow. Teens begin trying (trying!) to think for themselves, act on their own behalf, and make choices and changes in their lives.

This is the time to take advantage of this natural urge toward independence and *let them start taking responsibility.*

For the next few chapters, we will look at ways to help our teens grow up. We will organize these by *relationships*: what personal relationships are changing and what new relationships the student will be building: family relationships, friends, dating, work, and ministry. Finally, the homeschool high school student can start working on some serious, hard-core **socialization**.

Family Changes for the Homeschool High School Student

As the homeschooled high school student grows through the late teen years, family dynamics change rapidly. The habits of emotions and communication styles between parent and child seem to change overnight. *Seem to change,* because actually, these behaviors have been gradually shifting since puberty. We no longer relate to each other the same way anymore. When we recognize these natural shifts in the parent/teen relationship, we can avoid conflict and continue to build strong relationships through this process.

The most important principle to keep reminding ourselves, homeschool moms, is that **this separation process is healthy and natural.** This feels like giving birth all over again, only the labor pains last for years, and instead of a cute little infant, we receive loneliness and an empty bedroom. Well, that and the satisfaction of a job well done. Hey, we should have known this was what we were in for when we started two decades ago, right?

So how does this separation process affect the parent/teen relationship? What are some changing dynamics we can anticipate? How do we help our teens go through this change from *child* to *adult*? I do not claim to have all the answers (my teens would tell you that!), but I can share some guidelines that *greatly* ease our transitions with our own teens.

Teens may change favorite parents.

Now, we parents never play favorites, of course (*cough, cough*). However, during the growing up years, children tend to gravitate toward one parent or the other. Birth order, personality, common interests, or life experiences influence this relationship. For each of your children, you know which parent your child is most likely to confide in, confess to, and accept advice from. Moreover, if you have been homeschooling for several years, you, mom, may have become the "first choice parent" for most of your children.

However, during the teen years, this relationship could shift, particularly for boys. In our case, my oldest son and I were quite close during his growing up years because of our shared experiences (I had him very young, so I felt like we grew up together in many ways) and similar interests (we both like long arguments about abstract ideas). Beginning with puberty, he began naturally pulling away, until by late teens he would prefer to discuss heavy matters with his father first. I knew in my head that this was right and good: there was no one better in this world to teach my son how to man-up than his father. Yet it did, at times, feel like a loss. I had really treasured our talks, our confidences, our private jokes.

How to help

While I was feeling somewhat rejected, however, my husband was feeling more significance and satisfaction in his deepening relationship with our oldest as he became the role model and advisor. Seeing Dad take an active role helped me relax into the changes. I took a step back, offering to help or listen but not pushing myself on my son. Then when disagreements between my son and I arose (as they are sure to come when a hormonal mom and immature teen live together 24-7), I could gently encourage my son to seek his dad's opinion. Sometimes the same truth packaged in a more masculine answer made the lesson easier for the teen to appreciate.

On the other hand, my teen daughter is craving more mom time than ever. I must be careful to keep more margin in my day for the extra talking she needs, the spur-of-the-moment outings she proposes, and the teen girl dramas she needs to vent about. I am also on the lookout for new ways for us to spend time together doing our favorite girly things: attending concerts, serving in ministry together, doing housework, running errands, and even shopping. We have solved many world problems between clothing racks of the department store.

As parents, we may not realize how our personal relationships and communication patterns will change as teens grow. By recognizing this is a healthy, natural part of growing and not taking it personally, we can help our young people move into their new positions as *adults* in the family.

Teens communicate less.

This was another big adjustment for me. We are a *very* communicative family—this is one trait we all share. When we are excited, we are loud. When we are frustrated, we are loud. When we are learning, we're loud. When we are sad, we're loud. You can guess what happens when we are sick, upset, disagreeable, or angry (hint: the opposite of quiet).

As my teens grow older and begin thinking more independently, they become quieter. Well, not when they are angry. I hear less about what they are thinking, what they are feeling, what is happening with their friends, what they are dreaming about for the future. They start keeping their own counsel.

That can be good and can be bad. We worry about the bad part—becoming sullen, secretive, rebellious, or deceitful. What do we not know? That can seem terrifying. We can't control what we don't know, only they know it, and the cycle continues . . .

Guess what? *We cannot control our teens, anyway.* They are growing up. We can set house rules and homeschool deadlines, behavior expectations, and late-night curfews, but the end goal is still future independence. Our teens know instinctively that this really, truly is their own life, and they are preparing to live it without us. That starts with making up their own minds. Or trying to, anyway.

The more we push, the more we insist, the more we pry, the worse things get. Teens do not need judgment or nagging or criticism. They need wise advice, a patient ear (when they are ready), clear boundaries, and a safe place to practice adulting.

How to help

Mom, we need to stay available. We need to schedule less and hang around more. We can ask general, non-threatening questions and give them a chance to answer if they are ready. We should wait to ask when our teens want advice or a listening ear. We can find out what makes our teen ready to talk and create that environment regularly: a breakfast date, running errands, shopping trip, a quiet evening alone at home. Most of all, we can communicate more love and support than judgment and criticism. Make sure they know you are there to *help* not dole out discipline.

Teens are more emotional and argumentative.

Well, there is the whole hormone thing that has been wreaking havoc with your teen since puberty. It just does not seem to let up, especially for boys. It's not your imagination: hormones can be worse for boys, bless them.

Complicating the volatile emotions is this newfound mental independence, so now they have to openly question (mock, ridicule, disdain, debate) every other statement made in the house, no matter how trivial. If you, personally, are having a bad day and feel like you are at the end of your rope, your teen will find a particularly *stupid and inconsequential* molehill on which to stage his battle.

It is very, very hard not to take the bait and engage in a war of words. Because we know (oh, how we know!) that *they are so wrong!* As the parent, we should immediately *set them right! It's our job!* Sadly, engaging the hormonal, argumentative teen does not accomplish anything more than making everyone mad and ruining family dinner (not that I would know).

How to help

Do not engage. Try, as much as possible, to live peaceably with all teens. Ask if they are looking for answers or just voicing an opinion. Offer to help them find the answer. Even ask if they would like to research opposing viewpoints on that subject. Most of all, keep your cool. Home is where teens can be wrong and still be loved. Your own loved ones let you voice stupid errors and still respect you. None of us were half as brilliant when we were teens as we thought. As my father once wryly remarked, "When I was seventeen, my father didn't know anything, either."

Teens need less punishment.

Got your attention with that statement, didn't I? It is true. When our children were young, we spent a lot of time disciplining. Quite a bit of that discipline was punishment. "If you don't eat your vegetables, you have to eat them for breakfast." "If you don't go to bed the first time you're told, no bedtime story." "If you fight with your brother, you have to do his chores." We were giving time outs, we were taking away video games, we were making them scrub the walls. It is how we taught them right from wrong.

As teens grow, however, they need less punitive punishment and more consequences. Now is the time to start learning how the adult world works. When we do not shop up to work on time, we do not lose our bedtime story—we lose our job. When we do not pay our bills, we do not get a slap on the hand – we lose our car, house, or phone. Teens yearn for more freedom, so we must start by letting them take the responsibilities and the consequences.

They must finish their homework, or they'll get bad grades *and forfeit scholarship money,* money they will have to work harder to earn.

They must drive carefully because *they pay for their own car and insurance,* and after the first accident or ticket, rates rise drastically.

They must be home for curfew because *they will lose the car keys* otherwise.

They have to pay their phone bill on time *or their parents will repossess their phone.*

The older our children grow, the less we should need to be the bad guy. They have other authorities: the college financial office, the boss at work, the police, the ministry leader. Instead of coming down on them, we can remind them (not nag) and encourage them to keep up with their responsibilities. We should not stand over our teens with a whip and a stool to keep them in line. They will learn from the natural consequences of their behavior.

Our role as parents rapidly changes during these high school years. We go from the micromanaging, sometimes-nagging mom to encourager, counselor, friend, and first-responder. Yes, they are going to get in trouble. Yes, they will make mistakes. Yes, they will sometimes scare us. Nevertheless, these years are their last chance to practice adulting while at home, to try out responsibility and work ethic and building a reputation while they still have both parents right there at their side. Our challenge is to transition our relationship with our teens into a healthy one, respecting and recognizing their need to become adults.

Because truly, it is much harder for them than it is for us!

14. Developing New Friendships

My best friend is the one who brings out the best in me.
-- Henry Ford

THOUGH WE PARENTS NOTICE our teen's rapidly-changing relationship with us during the high school years, for your son or daughter, these relationships with **friends** represent the biggest social change. In fact, this growing need for friendship may be how your teen defines himself as a person during this period of his life.

Homeschool moms often have conflicting feelings about this urge for outside relationships. Accustomed to our somewhat isolated lifestyle as busy moms and homeschoolers, we may have such frantic schedules that we do not have a lot of close friends ourselves outside our immediate family. And we're doing fine, right? (Well, not exactly. But that's a conversation for my book *Rocking Ordinary*.)

Other teens are *so immature,* they can't be a great influence on our godly, talented, committed, exceptional young person, right?

Besides, our young person is so busy with studies, sports, work, music, volunteering, and ministry, what time does he have for hanging out with ne'er-do-well teens, anyway?

Life is not about having fun, after all.

But this is a harmful attitude to have, even if we're coming to it by accident. Maybe we aren't *trying* to isolate our homeschool teens, maybe we don't *mean* to make them lonely, maybe we aren't *purposefully* hindering them from developing relationships. Yet this can happen anyway if we don't intentionally take steps to help our young people develop friendships.

I'm not talking about getting your girl into the popular clique. And I'm not encouraging your son to spend more time on the streets. I am reminding all of us that since homeschoolers have the corner on socialization, we need to bring our A-game to the high school years.

Our teens should be developing meaningful relationships across the many spheres of their lives:

- personal friendships
- neighbors
- adult friends outside the family
- work associates
- church friends of differing ages
- ministry partners
- trusted mentors

One of the surprising things about our changing relationship with our teens is this shift away from being their sole resource for everything. As homeschool parents, we poured into our children nearly everything they knew – morally, academically, socially, practically. It is actually quite satisfying as they grow to look back and say, "I taught him everything he knows."

If our teens keep reaching out, they will build lasting relationships that matter.

Even as we homeschool during the high school years, teens are looking away from us for a different perspective. They want to know what other people think. They want to see differences of lifestyle, opinion, and beliefs. They want confirmation what they learned from us is indeed the way the world works.

Again, they want to try out adulting. They know instinctively that they are moving *away* from us soon, so they want to practice getting information, advice, and support from other sources. They are almost like different people from their parents (imagine that), and they want to establish their own relationships.

So the teen years give them an opportunity to learn about adult relationships through friendships and other relationships. By making friends of their own, they will learn valuable lessons we cannot teach them:

- how to resolve problems with someone outside the family,
- how to be loyal to a friend, and how to recognize who will be loyal to them,

- how to get advice from a friend, and how to know when and how to give advice, and
- how to discern the character of others

Outside friendships are very important for homeschool high school students. How can we help our teens make friends and influence people in a safe, productive way? Here are some tips that have helped me as a homeschooled teen (back in the day!) and that we use with our own teens now:

Remind teens that friends come in all ages and situations.

This is something we learn as adults, but most teens don't realize. Our closest friends may not live near us, look like us, worship with us, or have everything in common with us. My best friend lives clear across the country from me; we haven't lived near one another since I was a preteen. I enjoy a variety of friendships from different churches, different stages of life, and even different lifestyles (some don't homeschool!) One of my daughter's closest friends is two generations older than she is, besides her work associates and orchestra buddies.

A friendship is a close relationship that gives support and companionship through life. This is where homeschool teens have a distinct advantage: no longer confined to socialize within a small demographic, they are free to cultivate deep relationships within their community, their neighborhood, and their church.

Listen when your teen complains of loneliness.

Feeling alone is a common human emotion; we each struggle with it at times. You may even feel lonely right now, yourself. But when our teens complain that they don't have a close friend, it's tempting to brush their concern aside with a "you'll make friends later in life" or "successful people are usually lonely."

Those are true. We do need to develop the strength of character to stand alone in our convictions. There are seasons of life that are lonely, especially during major life changes like childbirth, moving, changing churches, and even starting to homeschool. Often times, friends we make in college and adulthood last longer than the pals we played with in our teens.

But our teens do need companionship now. They need to practice all those friend skills we mentioned before, and they need to learn the painful (and fun) friend lessons from the safety of home. So when they feel lonely, when they notice a void in their social life, it is important that we listen and take their concerns seriously.

Help your teen find new social outlets.

Just like there is more than one kind of friend, there is more than one way to make a friend. Sometimes, our teens just need some helping being creative. We can't mail-order a friend for them. And as I've learned from trial-and-error, setting up "play dates" to meet a new friend are not incredibly helpful, either. It doesn't help to set up our teens like a blind date. Just don't do it (spoken from experience).

Instead, we need to show our teen how to meet people the adult way: getting involved in the lives of others:

- join a ministry (or two),
- get a job,
- volunteer in the community,
- visit shut-ins,
- greet visitors,
- take a class, and/or
- join a sports team or music group.

Then keep doing it. Our teens will make friends and lose friends, break up with friends and become disillusioned with friends. But if they keep reaching out, they will build lasting relationships that matter.

Empower your teen by stepping back.

I asked my teen daughter what to say about teen friendships, what advice teens wished homeschool moms knew. Without missing a beat, she said, "Back off and let us grow up. A lot of homeschool moms just smother their teens. Like Mrs. X, the one who never lets her daughter go anywhere without her, so the teen just can't speak for herself. If her mother leaves the room, she's a different person! But no one can have a real relationship with her because her mom is attached to her hip. That's not healthy.

"But on the other hand, there are moms like Mrs. Z who don't parent enough. Teens need consequences, and they should just suffer for their own wrong choices. Parents who do what they say and live up to their own rules but let their teens develop their own relationships and make their own friend mistakes—homeschoolers need more parents like that."

Mom, let's back off. Let our teens practice friending without us. Then we'll be here when they need us, giving advice when they want it, and wiping the tears when they get hurt. Just like we will for the rest of their adult lives.

15. Dating

Love is patient and kind.
-- I Corinthians 13:4

I T MAY SEEM UNUSUAL that our series on homeschooling high school is spending so much time on these non-academic issues like family relationships and friendships and now dating. But if we step away from the transcripts a minute and look at what we're really doing here, we can't avoid talking about these important aspects of teen life.

Homeschooling is about training our teens for adult life, preparing them for the relationships and responsibilities that define who God created them to be. We cannot neglect these issues. Many times, they even affect our teen's attention to his academics. This is why we must understand these burgeoning relationships.

This includes their growing relationships with the opposite gender. Our teens, whether we like it or not, whether we are ready for it or not, whether we have strong feelings about it or not, have probably "noticed" boys and girls. They have a God-given urge to seek out a mate and enjoy the blessings of intimacy. They want love. This is a good thing, God says.

But obviously, like every other privilege God has given us, this blessing comes with responsibility: the responsibility of purity, of purpose, of discernment, of honor. It's our job as parents to prepare our young people for what will be the most important decision they ever make besides their decision to follow Christ.

Homeschooling is about training our teens for adult life, preparing them for the relationships and responsibilities that define whom God created them to be.

But first, I want to tell you to relax: I'm not going to get into a courtship vs. dating debate. I'm not going to prescribe a formula to follow. I'm not even going to cast judgment on all the "wrong" ways to teach these principles to our young people. Instead, I hope to show you how my husband and I discuss this issue with our teens. And whatever you call the process of learning about the opposite gender, making friends with boys and girls, and seeking God's will for a mate, we're going to call it all "dating" just for the sake of expediency. Perhaps we can take some of the fear and panic out of the issue and help you intentionally pass along your values to your teens.

Because this is the heart of homeschooling: passing on your beliefs and values to your next generation. Hopefully, when you set down your homeschool *why,* you didn't list specific salaries, titles, or external measures of behavior as your primary homeschool purpose. No matter what your most important homeschool values, I am fairly certain you are after *changed hearts and minds.* Right?

How We Talk To Our Teens About Dating

In our family, we don't have a one-time conversation with our teens, a sit-down in which we lay out all the rules and expectations and have them sign a contract. Some families chose to go that route (don't ask me how I know). For my husband and I, instead of a list of "thou shalt not's," we want to encourage our young people to seek God's will for their lives through their relationship with Him and others. That goes back to our family *why*.

Have continual conversations.

From the time they are young, we talk often about their future lives. We dream with them about how God might be using them, the ways He is already preparing them, the fun and exciting times ahead of them as adults. Of course, that includes their future families. And all the grandbabies they will give me. We can't leave that out!

Yes, they know that marriage is not always God's plan. But it is His norm (I Cor. 7). So this is what we expect for them until God reveals otherwise. Talking about their future families is a natural part of our conversation.

Respect God's standards.

From toddlerhood on, we are teaching our children how to treat others, what God's rules are for showing love and care to those around us: be kind, be obedient, be respectful, be sharing, be honest, etc. This includes issues of appropriateness. We teach them how to be modest. We teach them who to trust with personal information. We teach them appropriate levels of affection for family, friends, and strangers.

This conversation continues for teens. We have one level of physical and emotional affection for friends, and another for close family members. Until someone has moved beyond friendship closer to family status, those levels of intimacy aren't appropriate.

Of course, this applies to marital intimacy. There is a level of affection, emotional attachment, and physical bonding that is only appropriate in a marital commitment. When teens recognize this as a growth of the family relationship, it's something both precious to protect and exciting to anticipate.

Of course, when things get serious, it's time for a very specific conversation. When a teen or young adult begins dating, it's time to talk about exactly what *purity* means, what the house rules are, and what are the far-reaching physical, emotional, and spiritual consequences of inappropriate actions.

Give plenty of information.

We homeschool because we want to be our teen's primary source of education. Whatever our homeschool *why,* we have purposed to take on daily discipling and educating of this person. We can't be stingy about this information. By the teen years, it's time to generously inform our teens about sexuality and relationships.

I'm glad that my teens come to me during puberty and the teen years with their own questions about sexual health, birth control, abortion, and the opposite gender. I want to give them all the information I have. I am even happy to point them in the direction of more information if they need it. Their father and I are training them to take on responsibility for this

182

aspect of their lives just as much as everything else, so we welcome the opportunity to think through these issues with them.

And my teen daughter called me out for missing an opportunity recently. She needed a quick check up with her pediatrician for our foster care forms, proof that she was healthy and up-to-date on her own immunizations. She requested that I stay in the room with her for her physical exam. When she asked her pediatrician if she needed more shots, he told her that she was all up to date. "Except for Gardasil," he offhandedly referred to the vaccination against sexually transmitted infection. "But you probably don't want that one."

"Yeah, we don't need that, thanks," I replied.

"Wait a minute," my daughter's brow furrowed. "You didn't tell me about that. Why can't I get that shot? What's it for?"

I blushed, realizing my mistake in speaking for her without explanation. The doctor pulled out the fact-sheet and handed it to me, and I passed it immediately to her. I then explained why I felt she didn't need it, but that she was welcome to request it if she disagreed. She glanced at the sheet and asked the doctor a few questions about how the disease was transmitted, then declined it for the same reasons I expected. *She made an informed choice for herself.* That was far more important than my dictating her sexual health choices.

Make a difference between choice and rules.

As our teens approach adulthood, my husband and I have wrestled with their growing independence and our limited control. We've worked through the growing pains of launching young adults. Finally, we've come to an important realization: **we give them rules when they are home, but our young people must choose the adult they will become.**

We cannot—and should not – dictate their adult choices. We cannot – and should not – choose their beliefs, their mate, their occupation, their lives. We can disciple them, we can teach them, and we can demonstrate love to them. So, while they are in our home, they must abide by the house rules. Yet very, very quickly they are out of the house and must choose who they really are. If we are honest with our teens, we can build a trusting relationship.

This, then, is the principle we remind them. How they date, how they behave, how they work, how they play, how they live is not just *what they do* but really *who they are.* When they decide to pursue a relationship, when they wonder if they have met their match, when they consider how far they will or won't go before marriage, they are really defining **who they are before God and man.** Are they pure? Are they principled? Are they holy? Are they loving others? Are they selfish? Are they honorable?

Stay humble.

Years ago, a pastor advised my husband and me to never tell our teens how we got married because we eloped at a very young age. We have not followed that bad advice.

Instead, we answered our teens' questions openly and honestly about our past, both good choices and bad mistakes. We told them how and why we got married in a courthouse away from family and friends.

And we explained why they don't have to start their adult lives similarly alone and unsupported (you can read more about that story in my book *Rocking Ordinary*)

If we are honest with our teens, we can build a trusting relationship. We want them to come to us with their problems, to openly admit their mistakes, to let us help them face the difficult consequences. That will only be possible if we are humble and honest with them.

Be the parent.

It is still my job to ask questions. It is still dad's job to set the curfew. It is our job to enforce our standards and to set the expectation of family behavior.

We do need to draw the line. We have had the tough talks. They need to know where the protective fence is and what happens when they try to climb over it.

More than that, our teens must know how to make life decisions. There is no better opportunity for us to train them how to live for God and love others than during these exciting dating relationships.

Point them to biblical truth.

Too many dating and courtship resources attempt to twist Scripture to support their view. So when teens wrestle through their own faith issues as they become adults, this inconsistency with God's Word can seriously harm their view of Christianity, maybe even hinder their walk with God.

My husband and I are very careful to lift up God's standards for love and marriage while remaining respectful of the diverse ways God works in human affairs. Yes, God miraculously led Abraham's servant to find Isaac's wife. And He beautifully created Eve to perfectly complement Adam. But Jacob chose his own spouse, Joseph married the pagan priest's daughter (and birthed blessed sons by her), and Ruth herself pursued Boaz for a husband. And yet, Jesus Christ's earthly family also included a harlot, David's wife after an illicit affair, pagan foreign spouses, and other seemingly less-than-ideal pairings.

187

God never provided one simple way to find the ideal spouse. Instead, He chose to make the entire process fun, exciting, a little dangerous, and very romantic. And each relationship, He promised to redeem for His purpose.

I am the luckiest girl in the world, married over two decades to a hot Latino who spoils me every day. We've had our loud fights, our financial woes, and our sleepless nights, but I wouldn't trade my life with him for anything in the world.

And my prayer every day for my children is that they, too, will be married happily ever after.

16. Work and Service

Far and away the best prize that life has to offer is the chance to work hard at work worth doing.
--Theodore Roosevelt

HOMESCHOOL PARENTS KNOW that *adulthood* is the entire purpose of our teaching. We are working hard to put ourselves out of a job. If we do this right, our students leave and never (or rarely) come back, right?

Yet we too easily forget that goal in the thick of homeschooling. We are buried in classes and tests, workbooks and transcripts, and we completely lose sight of the end game: responsible adulthood.

This is where work and ministry come in. By making responsibility and service a part of our teen's high school years, we set the stage for the rest of his

189

life. When we help our teen transition into both, we find valuable opportunities to train him for a lifetime of serving and giving.

When we looked at what our teen does year by year in chapter 3, we listed milestones like working a job and serving in ministry right alongside academics and social development. Working and serving are important skills our teen can begin developing if we are intentional during these high school years.

Learning to Work

Your teen has likely been working his whole life . . . right here at home. You gave him chores and responsibilities from the time he could walk, so he already knows about responsibility. High school is the perfect time to build on this understanding.

At Home

While life outside the house becomes increasingly attractive and busy, teens easily begin to start slacking off on the usual chores at home. Now is the time to renew room inspection each morning, reminding teens they need to pick up the laundry, clear off the dresser, and make the bed each day. Be sure he has other chores, too: yard work, vacuuming, bathroom duty, and/or dishes.

With Finances

Perhaps during the middle school years, your child may have begun finding odd jobs for spare cash. If not, now is the perfect time to start instigating that behavior. It is not your job as the parent to find him a job. Create the need for a job. Make him want to work so badly that he gets the job himself.

How do we create this need? My husband and I cut off the gravy train early. We don't give spending money, petty cash, or small trinkets. We don't purchase expensive electronics, phones, or game subscriptions. We don't even buy our teens more than the bare minimum clothing items. We make the default answer to "can I have . . ." always "when you buy it." Very quickly, our teens want the money to provide themselves with what they desire.

Does this sound cruel and unusual? It shouldn't. As parents, we work hard – very hard – to provide the necessities of food, clothing, shelter, and love to our family. As homeschoolers, we've sacrificed even more to personally pass on education, training, and experiences that shape the incredible young people they are. Most of us have made the decision to live on a single income. Now, our teens are not wise enough to rise up and call us blessed yet, but one day, maybe.

Until then, the gravy train is their responsibility. The answer to all of these questions in our house is the same:

- Can I have a car?
- May I get a phone?
- Can I go shopping?
- Will you buy me a souvenir?
- May I go to the fair?
- How will I pay for college?

The answer? "Get a job and save your money." After a while, they get tired of hearing the same thing all the time, so we don't get asked much anymore. They just work hard and save up.

Letting them take the initiative

Each of our teens found their own jobs when they got desperate enough. This is hard when they were younger because many businesses won't hire young people before age fifteen or sixteen. "Necessity is the mother of invention," the proverb says, so if we allow our teens to do without for long enough, they will find a way.

Our teens have worked as referees (after getting licensed), babysitters, yard workers, pet sitters, paper trimmers, and lemonade delivery boys. They have worked for family, friends, neighbors, and church members. They found their neighborhood the best place to drum up work (even going house to house), and they learned the value of a good reputation for securing repeat business and referrals.

Setting expectations

With the privilege of working follows the responsibilities of managing expectations. Young employees and entrepreneurs in our home have some guidelines to help them build healthy work habits:

- Schoolwork and household chores always come first.
- The teen alone handles all interviews and all work-related communication; Mom and Dad never get involved.
- Transportation is tricky, but it remains the teen's responsibility. If he needs a ride from parents, he asks each time and does not assume. His work transportation needs cannot interfere with his parents' responsibilities.
- If his work transportation becomes a burden (like when the job is more than a few minutes away), the teen finds a way to compensate, perhaps by doing extra chores.

To some parents, these guidelines sound harsh, but this way, our teens pay for their work transportation. One son realized that refereeing games an hour away would cost too much gas money for his parents, so he declined them. He takes games he can bike to, instead, so he can keep all his earnings. Our daughter's job is twenty minutes away, and she needs a ride to and from work, so she does extra household chores and cooking that day to free up my time.

By the junior year of high school, a regular part-time job tremendously benefits the teen. No matter how menial, how boring, or how grueling, this job teaches teens a valuable perspective they need before entering adulthood:

- work is hard,
- fellow employees are sometimes difficult,
- jobs and salaries are valuable,
- character and work ethic are rare and valued, and
- bills are difficult to pay, and luxuries are not always worth the extra expense.

Learning to Serve

Teens can become notoriously self-centered. There's just something about this stage of life that renders young people unduly egocentric and selfish. We should anticipate this to some extent, but our job is to help them mature beyond this. We want to see our teens grow into compassionate, caring, serving adults who demonstrate Christ-like, servant leadership in their personal relationships.

This is why it is imperative we keep our young people serving God. They need to recognize the needs outside their interests, the people outside their circle of friends and reach out in love. How do we instill a love of service in our teens?

Serve together

We can't pass on a habit we don't practice. This is true of our personal walk with the Lord, and it's true of Christian service. The first step in getting our teens involved is making sure we are serving the Lord in our churches and communities:

- get involved in a ministry or two at church,
- instead of saying "someone should," take the lead and do it,
- volunteer in the community for causes you care about, and
- get involved as a family – do it together!

Ideas for family service

Maybe you are in between ministries or looking for a fresh idea how to serve as a family. Here are some ideas that have worked for us:

Take them along. When I led a mid-sized music ministry in an East Coast church, I took my young children with me constantly. They played with dolls and cars on the floor of my office while I filed music. They played pretend instruments or sang along with the choir in rehearsals. They napped under the piano during lessons. They were constantly there, so they became friendly with the church members working with me.

Teach them how to serve. My husband directs our church's AWANA program, and he's using it as an opportunity to train our teen daughter, along with other young people, how to teach and disciple children. This year, our daughter teaches the Bible lesson, plans crafts, and supervises games for preschoolers.

Expect continual service. There isn't really a question of "do you want to serve the Lord" in our family – it's expected. Each Sunday, if we are not sick, we should be doing something, every one of us, to help those around us in the cause of Christ. If you have an instrument, play it. If they need a nursery worker, hold a baby. If they ask for a sound assistant, learn how to do it. There's always something that needs to be done.

Make it a family affair. Reaching out to the community is also important to us, and we try to involve the entire family in the efforts. Whether we are donating to the Salvation Army, packaging food in the food pantry, or organizing a block party, everyone works together. Even as we prepared for adoption, there was plenty for all of us to do. It is always more fun to serve together!

These two issues -- working and serving -- go hand-in-hand. Teens grow up to realize they need to provide for their own needs and then reach out to give to those around them. This is part of being a mature adult. As homeschool parents, we have a great opportunity to make these lessons a priority in our teaching.

17. Teen Driving and the Scary World out there

Never lend your car to anyone
to whom you have given birth.
--Erma Bombeck

WHILE OUR TEENS ARE BUSY completing courses and filling up transcripts, they are fast becoming young adults, taking giant strides out the door of our home into the exciting adult world them.

This hits home dramatically when our teen earns his first driver's license. Yes, we take them out practicing and celebrate their first vehicle and take pictures of them holding their new license, but meanwhile, our hearts are screaming, "NO! Don't go! Don't drive away just yet!" Nevertheless, drive away they must, out into the wild blue yonder (or maybe into the mailbox).

I handled my oldest son's driving quite well. I wisely bowed out of teaching him behind the wheel; his grandmother and father did that. I am your gal for book learning and museum wandering; I'm not the one you want yelling and clawing at the dashboard. So our son took his course online and practiced on the road with patient, calm family members who had good life insurance policies. I did ride with him an hour away for his final driving test . . . then sobbed all the way home. Like I said, I took it well.

It is not hard for a homeschool student to get a driver's license. With a few phone calls to the department of motor vehicles and some web research, we found that taking the course online and learning to drive with a parent was the least expensive and simplest way to go. When he arrived at the DMV for his learner's permit, his father accompanied him to provide insurance and driving instruction information, and I brought along my teacher lesson plan book to prove his homeschool status. I signed a form saying our son was, indeed, a full-time student; his father signed a few more about liability and insurance and other legalities. The teen took a test on a computer, then he was awarded his permit.

Different states have different requirements, though, so check your DMV website or call ahead. Particularly ask about their proof of education; I found out later I merely needed to sign a form saying my student attended homeschool.

After that, it was just a matter of tracking the student's driving time. As we felt our way through the driving experience with our oldest, we stumbled upon a few guidelines that we have since codified as the law for driving in our house:

Teens may not drive the family minivan. This was my first decree, and I was so adamant about it that I was able to push the law into unanimous ratification. That one vehicle represents the only transportation that will fit the entire family; if anything happened to it, we could not so much as get to church. So don't even ask, you aren't getting the keys.

Teens have to acquire their own vehicle to learn on. With my minivan out of the picture, that leaves usually drives it to work every day. So our oldest was forced to look elsewhere. Fortunately for him, his grandparents were in the process of purchasing a new vehicle, so he bought a used truck with high mileage but a great track record inexpensively. His siblings are so jealous.

Our daughter, on the other hand, has been looking for her car ever since her brother's great deal. She's also been saving her money in a large jar labeled CAR FUND. I've caught her eyeing used cars on our street and asking adults if they are thinking about getting a new vehicle. It's quite amusing. Lately, she's even been talking with her dad about leasing his sedan from him.

Teens must pay for their own vehicle costs, including insurance. The car insurance was a huge concern for my husband and me until we had the great epiphany that *it wasn't our responsibility.* That took a big load off our minds and wallets. My husband, out of the goodness of his heart, did a lot of research for our son, however. He found a few cut-rate companies, but teen boys are still expensive to insure. THEN he learned that some insurance companies allow policyholders to insure *the vehicle, not the driver.* Until the first ticket or accident, there is no additional charge for the additional driver, just for his car. However, once the teen has an accident, his rates go way up. Our compromise was to carry the truck on our insurance and allow the teen to pay us the difference. Once he has an accident or ticket, he must get his own car insurance. That has been a powerful motivator to keep him driving carefully.

Teen drivers pay for all gas, tires, oil changes, and maintenance. Driving and owning a vehicle is a tremendous responsibility, and providing for those costs are difficult for a teen. This keeps them working hard, budgeting finances, and maintaining the vehicle. It may have a lot of McDonald's wrappers, Sonic cups, and stinky ball caps littered inside it, but that truck is well-loved and cared for.

It is scary when teens drive off. Will they come home? When? Will they get into trouble? How much?

Finding a balance between protecting and empowering, teaching and training, discipline and grace are never so difficult as when letting the teen drive. A few reminders helped me stay (relatively) calm:

It is time to let them practice adulting. Teens cannot grow up unless we allow them to practice being responsible. They must drive off, stand on their own, and choose what kind of person they will be.

Their character is revealed when we are not looking. I always knew that in my head, but when my teen son drove away from the house all day, that was when I learned *who he really was.* The scary thing is that everyone else gets to see his true character first: his employer, his friends (and friends' parents), and local business owners. Regardless, we must allow our teens to demonstrate who they are; they need to find their standards for themselves.

We are still the parents. Yes, the ability to drive changes so much; overnight, the teen takes large steps out the door. However, they are still teens living under our house with dependent status. We are still the older, wiser providers in the relationship. It's important for everyone in the family to remember that.

We can – and should – enforce curfew by taking away keys. We can – and should – enforce financial responsibilities by repossessing unpaid items. We can – and should – ensure household chores are completed, family relationships are respected, and schoolwork is completed. Now is not the time for anyone to slack off.

Teen driving represents a huge milestone in your young person's life – and in yours. With grace, guidelines, and some absorbent tissues, you will survive this stage and maybe even look back at it fondly.

18. College or Not

A thorough knowledge of the Bible is worth more than a
college education.
-- Theodore Roosevelt

AFTER SEVERAL YEARS of bucking the educational system, many homeschool families find traditional college education difficult to imagine. Why return to the classroom? Do students truly need another four years or more of education and tens of thousands of dollars of debt before beginning real life?

My own teens ask the same question. Actually, my older two briefly considered the possibilities but quickly came to the conclusion that college is right for them. My oldest son is pursuing a degree at Liberty

209

University. My high school daughter is considering several careers that all require a college degree.

Our next son disagrees with the entire idea of college. He aspires to the simple pleasures of life – a low-stress job, simple house, and beautiful wife who is a great cook and can drive him around (as a preschooler, he used to ask me privately which pretty teen girls at church had driver's licenses). He often says he will work at a bank every day like his father and come home for dinner.

However, there is a wrinkle in his plan: he could not support a family on a teller's salary, and that's the only banking position he can obtain without a degree.

My husband and I have strong feelings about college, mostly because we are both college dropouts. Our twenties were extremely difficult for that reason. We quickly found ourselves hungry, broke, desperate, and in debt with young mouths to feed and few prospects. For over a decade, my husband worked two jobs to keep groceries on the table, and even while homeschooling little ones, I worked in and out of the home to keep the children in shoes. Life was very difficult.

Thanks to hard work, persistence, and the grace of God, my husband David now has a great job and a strong resume. Yet if he were starting now, he could not get the job he has; all the upper-level jobs in banking are now closed to young people with no business degree.

Many other fields are similar: business, medicine, finance, education, the arts, even sports fields require education and training in addition to experience. Some notable careers do not require a four-year degree, but the majority of those would still require some training or certification. There remains a wage issue; if a young adult is planning to support a growing family, the paycheck for many of these careers would place a family of four in the low-income bracket.

On the other hand, many of us *have* made a nice life for ourselves without a degree. I have enjoyed great opportunities in publishing and music. My husband has started a soccer club in his spare time besides bank management. We have friends who are entrepreneurs, business owners, and even executives . . . all without higher education.

I asked my friends on Facebook what they thought about this issue, and they gave a variety of responses. Most of those were great reminders to let the teen take the lead, keep the conversation positive, and encourage long-term thinking. A few of my friends are against college outright, but most parents seem to desire more education for their homeschool graduates. Whatever your own personal opinions, there are several principles we can all agree on.

Young adults do not need to accumulate debt.

Student debt is the number one reason homeschoolers object to a college education. I have never heard anyone say, "Young people don't need more larnin'." Usually, the argument is that the cost outweighs the benefit. **The high cost of college need not prohibit our students from learning.**

Avoiding college debt is a major part of our college conversation at home. We know from

212

experience how debt cripples young families, and we emphasize this to our own teens. They need to prepare themselves to get through college without jeopardizing their future by accumulating debt.

Young homeschool graduates do not need to be thrown into paganism.

This is the second greatest objection to college after homeschooling: on campuses across the country, the faith and worldview of our young people are under attack. After years of carefully sheltering and training our children, we do not need them to be disillusioned and confused by every class and friend they meet.

Community college and even state schools are so tempting – several are located within driving distance of our home. As soon as those ACT scores are released, universities across the country send swag and large envelopes to our students to entice them into enrolling.

However, **going away to college is our young adult's first steps toward living on his own**. He is out of the house and on his own, away from the watchful eye of mom and the patient reminders of dad. We quickly realized that our students needed some training wheels, a crutch to help them learn how to provide for themselves, make their own choices, live up to their own character, and try adulting on for size . . . but with that support and even rules to make sure they couldn't fall too far.

Considering those reasons, we made it easy for our students to choose that safety net. We told our teens that though they are personally responsible for their own college tuition wherever they attend, if they attend a Christian university we will pay room and board.

We allow our students to choose their own university, however. Our oldest chose Liberty University, which is more liberal in many ways than our own home and church. But after visiting with him, we agree that it is a good intermediary step toward living on his own. He has the freedom to choose what is right and the restrictions to keep him from getting into too much trouble. And, as he reminds me often, "I'm in church services or Bible classes *all the time!*" He attended on campus for one year and then returned home to complete his degree there online.

Young adults need to learn how to provide for themselves.

Many of my friends on Facebook mentioned a gap year – a period of time in which their teen stayed home to work and to investigate options for college and career. This is becoming increasingly common.

I agree these experiences are valuable and necessary, which is why we built gap year into the senior year of high school. By that time, the student must be working at least part time (our oldest worked full time through his entire senior year). In addition, he should be planning specifically for his future:

- what are his goals for the next five years,
- how he will provide for his own food, clothing, and shelter,
- how he will provide for his future spouse and family, and

- if he attends college, what possible careers his degree supports, and if he doesn't land his first-choice career, what other options he has.

Remember, the teen should complete the core high school classes early in the high school years; by the end of his junior year, most homeschool students have completed the minimum requirements for graduation. This allows the senior year to be lighter academically. That is an important component of gap year: students need some experience working and going to classes simultaneously, too. This is what the next stage of their life will look like.

If our young men are not going to school full time, they need to either find their own place to live or continue to pay their bills until they do so. They are growing up and moving on now – it is time to spread those wings and leave the nest, birdies!

Young people need to think through these issues themselves.

Taking these first steps into adulthood is scary, no matter how ready our young people are to graduate.

216

Actually, I think the more mature and levelheaded they are, the scarier this seems because they realize the tremendous responsibility they are taking on.

However, this is their own life. We should not *force* them to go to college (or the university of our own choice), and we cannot *choose* what career they will take. This is the time for them to make their own life choices and forge their own path. Here are some more principles to make this decision easier, at least for you:

- Have short, casual conversations often, instead of a few highly charged lectures.

- Ask questions, like "what do you imagine your life like when you are my age?" or "what do you do (other than play video games) that excites you?" or even "what high school course do you hate the least?"

- Keep them working and paying bills. Teens think their first job makes them rich . . . until they see how fast they can use up a paycheck.

- Encourage them to ask other adults about their career and education.

- Be honest about your own college experience, the good and the bad, and what you wish you had done differently.

Remember that their life will radically change between ages 21, 31, and 41. Look at how different yours is now from when you first started out, and allow God to lead them graciously into their own unique path.

19. Choosing a College

An investment in knowledge pays the best interest.
-- Benjamin Franklin

IF YOUR HIGH SCHOOL STUDENT is considering college, he will need to decide which colleges to apply to. And if your high school doesn't want to go to college, he should still work through this process along with you to decide which is his least-hated school, just in case he changes his mind. Picking favorite schools, applying for admissions, finding scholarships, and determining a financial plan take time and effort. Most teens are not highly motivated to even think about these issues, let alone do the paperwork.

But that's why we are the parents, to make them do things they don't want to do.

There are three questions that will help guide you and your student toward the right college:

- What career, interest, or ministry is God likely leading him toward?
- What are educational or philosophical priorities most important to your family?
- What campus culture fits the student best?

The intersection of these three areas contains a smaller group of schools that fit your student best. It's the sweet spot of colleges that he will seriously consider and compare. But just like homeschooling philosophy or curriculum, it's not the same for every student. That's why you'll want to help your student think through these issues.

For example, I'll show you how our first son walked through the process of choosing his college.

1. Identify a major or school of learning

My oldest son Gian always knew he wanted to study the sciences, though his specific interests changed over the years. In middle school, he was into astronomy and considered studying astrophysics in college. In much of high school, his interest was in geology; he wanted to be the next John Morris, a highly respected creationist geologist. But when he learned that actually, geologists don't spend all day every day standing a little too close to volcanos or showing people pictures of themselves next to volcanoes, but rather worked long hours in labs organizing rocks, he lost interest. By his senior year, however, he was completely in love with math.

Could he make a living as a mathematician? Well, actually, yes, quite easily, as a matter of fact. A quick internet search found multiple career opportunities with more than sufficient starting income. So it was decided: math it is. His only stipulation was that college math must be new and different from high school math, which bored him.

Now he knew he needed a college with a strong math program, and preferably a respected school of science. He asked a few scientists he respected for recommendations to start his list of prospective schools.

2. Set the school parameters.

This is where we as parents weighed in. We strongly advised our son to get his undergraduate degree from a *Christian* university. This was his first experience living away from home and his first time taking classes outside his house. We felt a Christian campus was a good way to transition from homeschooling to academia and real life. He can learn in a college environment without questioning if the faculty has his best interests at heart – academically, morally, and spiritually. Also, he could practice living on his own within protective rules. To sweeten the incentive, we offered to pay room and board at the Christian college of his choice.

Since he was looking for a degree in the sciences, considering higher education afterward, and perhaps pursuing a career in academia, we advised him to choose an *accredited* school.

Those were his only two parameters: Christian and accredited. He had his own financial considerations since he was solely responsible for tuition.

3. Consider campus culture.

From recommendations of friends and the names of Christian colleges his dad and I knew off hand, Gian already had a small list of schools from which to choose. He did his own internet research to add to the list. Then he began looking out college websites and contacting admissions offices.

From internet stalking, though, he learned a lot about the culture of the schools, and that quickly clarified the choice in his mind. He realized that having certain amenities and opportunities were important to him. He also learned that he had preferences for student body size. He did not realize those aspects were important to him until he started looking at their websites and brochures, getting a feel for how colleges advertised themselves.

Gian determined he wanted to study in a large school that offered state of the art technology and a variety of student experiences and opportunities. He wanted to ensure the student body itself contained diverse demographics. Finally, he wanted the science school, itself, to be highly respected, having faculty with frequently published research.

Once he recognized his campus preferences, on top of his choice of major and our family parameters, Gian had narrowed down the thousands of colleges in America to a short list of only two or three possibilities. Very quickly, one rose to the top of his list.

He was fairly certain he had found his school of choice, but he needed to make sure. After all, he had not yet visited a single college campus yet. By this time, however, he had talked with the admissions offices of his top schools, obtained financial and admissions information from them, and even spoken faculty at his favorite school. Now it was time to visit.

Many colleges and universities provide opportunities for high school students to visit. Our son signed up for "College for a Weekend" on campus the fall of his senior year. Since we had never seen this college for ourselves, his father and I flew there with him. We toured the campus, speaking with several faculty and students over an afternoon, then we left Gian to stay for the weekend and we drove away, confident he would make the right decision for himself.

How to Help Your Teen Decide

I think the college decision is a little scary. We want to see our teens make the right choice, and we want college to be a good experience. We have our own college experiences to learn from, both good and bad. We want to ensure our students do not make the mistakes we did. How can we protect our young adults?

1. Keep college in perspective.

There are some truly big, scary decisions in life. Like whether to wholeheartedly follow the Lord and marriage. Stuff like that changes lives forever.

College is a little below that. Yes, there are horror stories about young people who have given up on their faith or sunk themselves financially because of bad college decisions. Quite frankly, most college mistakes don't have to ruin lives. Our young people will make mistakes. They will even sin. And they will learn from all of it. Choosing a college will not send them to hell. How they handle the decision and the results are what ultimately matters.

2. Choose few battles.

Some parts of the college experience will scare you more than others. Like maybe the spiritual battle or the financial hardship. Find your one or two main ones, and make *those* your big deals. This is why we chose *Christian college* and *you pay your own bills without loans.* Those are the rules because abandoning the faith or going into deep debt are really the only ways we define college failure.

3. Let him choose.

College is a big decision, but young adults need decision-making practice. It can be scary to leave such an important life choice to an immature teen, but our young people will not become mature without experience. We can give them this experience by letting them choose their college.

4. Let him take charge.

After he has chosen his school(s) to which he will apply, let him take over communication with the university. He can contact the admissions office himself, reach out to faculty members, and ask his own questions. Speaking up for himself is an important skill he will need on campus.

5. Let them pay.

College is wickedly difficult to pay, for now, exponentially harder than when we were students. As the saying goes, "Life is hard, and then you die."

Do not spring your financial expectations on your student all of a sudden. Make sure he knows all through high school that he needs to pay for his education, or what part of his bill he will assume. Remind him often that his grades mean money when it comes to scholarships (he will not believe you, but he will learn). In addition, keep reminding him when he gets his job that he needs to save for those first bills.

As soon as he decided what college to attend, Gian began the application process. And as soon as he was accepted, he began paying his bill. It sobered him up quickly to see his bank account drained so fast.

6. Let him go.

Driving away to college, whether across town or across the country, is a huge step into adulthood. Suddenly, faculty and staff treat your young person as an adult, with adult responsibilities and expectations. Taking care of his own academic, social, financial, and physical responsibilities prepares him for a lifetime of adulthood.

This is the time for us to take a big step back. We are not looking over his shoulder anymore. We cannot clean up his messes or even tell him he has spinach in his teeth (is he even brushing his teeth?!). Now it is time to pray, offer advice (on the rare occasions he will call home), and watch God turn our young person into the adult he was always created to be.

20. Transcripts

Big jobs usually go to the men who prove their ability
to outgrow small ones.
-- Theodore Roosevelt

Finally, we approach one of the most-asked questions for homeschooling high school: **how do we produce a transcript.** When I first asked my friends what was their top homeschool high school question, this was the number one concern. Preparing a high school transcript sounds intimidating, official, and scary.

Guess what? Transcripts are not hard at all. Just to prove it, I will give you a **free sample transcript you can use** at the end of this chapter.

Making your student's transcript is the single easiest high school task. Seriously, you cannot mess this up. To help you understand, I will hold your hand all the way through the process. Here we go.

One of the scariest things we do as homeschool parents is imagining graduation. How do we know if our homeschool high school student is finished? Are we sure we did enough? Did he complete enough credits? What in the world should that transcript look like, anyway?

Preparing a high school transcript is not, as it turns out, rocket science. It was nearly rocket science when I graduated from my basement homeschool *mumble, mumble* years ago. Today, it is hard to find a college or university in America that has not admitted homeschool students already; many top schools are even actively recruiting homeschoolers.

This is not an exaggeration, as I feared when our turn came last year. When my oldest son neared graduation, I was unsure how prospective colleges would receive his transcripts and test scores. As it turned out, I need not have feared: once his ACT scores (along with his grades and classification as *homeschool student*) hit admissions office desks, our phone started ringing off the hook. No joke, we could not get them to stop calling and sending full-color brochures.

This was not just his top-pick schools, either. Ivy League colleges would not take *no* for an answer for months but kept calling and mailing and emailing and begging him to just give them a chance. In frustration, he asked Cornell why they wouldn't leave him alone. The recruiter told him, **"Because you are a minority who was homeschooled and likes math. We need that."**

In spite of the fact public and private students are finding college acceptance increasingly competitive and scholarships harder to obtain, homeschool students who work hard and produce objective measurements of aptitude find universities eager to work with them.

Demonstrate hard work

By hard work, I mean seriously do the homework. Homeschool high school students still need to complete or exceed their state's minimum requirements for graduation. In our homeschool, my students complete the minimum requirements mandated by our state by the end of the junior year. By the end of the senior year, they exceed the requirements for a distinguished achievement program.

In addition to academics, homeschool high school students should pursue outside interests to demonstrate work ethic. Performance groups, competitive sports, volunteer hours, and part-time jobs show universities the student is willing to put muscle and sweat into his own future.

Provide objective measurements

By objective measurements, I mean other than the parents who obviously love them very much. Homeschool high school students should pursue other opinions on their work and life skills to corroborate their grades. My teens take a few challenging classes online, and the grades they receive are similar to those they make on mom-graded projects; this gives another layer of objective proof. Similarly, standardized tests (like the college entrance exams) should represent aptitude in the same vicinity as school grades. If a student scores a 19 on the ACT but turns in a 4.0

transcript, the admissions office will wonder why this does not match.

In addition, homeschool high school students should have cultivated working relationships with adults outside the home who can recommend their work ethic and character. This is another reason extra-curricular program like sports and music, ministry opportunities, volunteer work, and regular employment are so valuable for homeschoolers. These recommendations will provide another layer of objective testimony about the student's abilities.

Begin transcripts early

At the beginning of our high school journey, I did an internet search for my state's public school requirements for graduation. Then I planned my tentative high school course so I would have a clear picture of where we were headed. Finally, I began a working transcript. At the end of each semester, I added grades and course descriptions.

For my first transcript, I created a simple form in Google documents. I started this during my son's freshman year by listing the courses he was taking and the grades he earned. At the end of each semester, I updated the doc with his grades and included a course description starting on the next page. Finally, I shared the document with him, giving him "read only" permission so he could see his progress and grade point average.

When it came time to apply to his first-choice college, he did most of the paperwork himself. And now when he needed a transcript, I was ready for him. I quickly viewed the university's sample homeschool transcript and found they wanted even fewer details on a one-page transcript. With the information at my fingertips, I spent a quick twenty minutes making a simple transcript for them. Easy peasy!

Free Homeschool High School Transcript Form!

Want help starting your student's homeschool high school transcript? Here's the easiest form you'll ever keep. Just give me your email address, and I'll send it right to you. Keep it updated each semester, and by senior year, you are ready to go! Simply visit **lagarfias.com/transcripts**.

21. College Entrance Tests

One test of the correctness of educational procedure is the happiness of the child.

-- Maria Montessori

BESIDES CREATING A TRANSCRIPT, navigating college entrance exams is the next scariest issue for homeschooling high school. Parents and teens are understandably nervous because a lot of money is riding on the results of these tests.

Let me say right up front: this is another opportunity to keep a wise perspective on our homeschooling. **No single test can measure the value of your homeschool.** Write that down, and post it in your lesson plan book, on your white board, on the refrigerator, and on your first born son's face. **The**

value of your homeschool is infinitely greater than the sum of any test score.

You'll forget that, just like I do. We lose sight of our homeschool *why* sometimes, and we forget that all-encompassing purpose that led us to teach our children at home – to take on the responsibility and privilege of educating our student counter-culturally. For most of us, this was not an economic decision. We did not decide to homeschool our child so we could raise the next billionaires, so they could win millions on TV's Jeopardy, or even so they could secure thousands of dollars in college financial aid. Right? We are homeschooling because we pray they will become unique adults, because of the relationship we yearn to cultivate in their hearts, and because of the commitment to God and others we want to inspire.

No matter how stressful the college entrance exams may be, no matter how confusing, tricky, or frustrating this process is for us and for our students, it is vital we keep our end game in mind. Satan would like nothing more than to distract us from the character issues at stake. The world would like nothing more than to convince us that the dollars are the most important. And our own pride is so tempted to work hard for the points and the glory. We must not fall for it -- we are close to the finish line. Let us continue our race with patience and faith.

That said, most of our students *will* need to pass through the valley of the shadow of testing before they graduate from high school. And in the interest of full disclosure, I have to tell you the truth: it's really not that bad. Back in the dark ages, before homeschoolers were common representatives in testing facilities, I still managed to survive, earning a top score. I passed on much the same strategies to my son, who is not a natural test-taker, and he still earned a respectable grade and won some financial aid and Ivy League recognition. You can do this, I promise.

How do you help your student prepare for what may be the most important test he ever takes? Here's my plan for test success.

1. Relax.

Seriously, I can *not* emphasize this enough. The more you relax about this test, the more your student will relax. This is so important because your teen's mind doesn't work well under stress. The test questions will require quick thinking, creative problem solving, and sharp instincts – three mental abilities that are hindered under pressure. If you keep your cool in the months leading up to the test, your student is more likely to remain close to his peak mental capabilities.

More importantly, this test is a tremendous opportunity for you as a parent to teach a valuable life lesson. Though there are high-pressure moments that do define the direction of our lives, the real test is how we handle the pressure and the outcome. The test day isn't really what you are preparing your student for. You are really preparing him for *how to handle his results*.

2. Focus on core subjects.

Whether you take the ACT or the SAT, the majority of the test deals with the core subjects students work on throughout high school. The single best way to prepare your student is by providing a strong English and math foundation in the first two years of high school.

Your student needs to know the rules of grammar, usage, and punctuation instinctively. He should recognize sentences and know how to fix fragments and run-ons. He should also be aware of basic paragraph structure, how to recognize good writing, and how to fix poor development.

Your student also needs a strong understanding of algebra. He should have memorized the basic rules and functions of algebraic equations. He should know what is the right way to solve for inequalities and quickly recognize illogical or sloppy equations. He also should have a working knowledge of geometry functions and have memorized formulas for areas and volumes of different shapes. Even if he has not yet taken trigonometry or precalculus, he should have been introduced to some basic ideas like sin/cosine/tangent and what those ratios mean.

3. Choose the right test for your student.

I naturally gravitate to the ACT; it's the test I took, and it just makes so much sense to me. Yet we still did some research before choosing the right test for our student.

Check the university. For his top pick schools, our son researched what tests they accepted. All of his favorites allowed students to submit whichever test they preferred. We also learned that his top choice school didn't even read the writing portion of the ACT. So it would have been a complete waste of time to prepare for that portion of the exam. This immediately took a load off his mind.

Try tests on for size. Both tests provide free sample tests online. This is a great benefit for students who are unsure which is right for them. Have your student take one of each and see which gives him a better grade. Find the sample ACT test and the sample SAT online.

4. Let him study ahead of time.

Once your student has chosen a test, encourage him to begin preparing. Ideally, he should study daily, but at least weekly. Again, leave this in his hands. The test is for him, not for you!

Each testing company offers sample questions and study materials online, both free and paid. Your public library also has free study guides. You will need to reserve them ahead of time, though, because all the teens in town are after them.

5. Take the test early.

Register your teen to take the test his junior year. This allows him to finish two full years of high school, making the test material familiar. This also gives him plenty of time to retest later, if he wishes.

6. Allow the student to retest.

In our homeschool, we purchase the first test and study materials from the test publisher for the student. If the teen wants to retest, he can pay for it himself. This gives students an additional financial incentive to study, and it also teaches them valuable lessons about investing in their future.

Our son, for instance, received good but not outstanding scores his first try. His math and science scores were very good, but his reading score was abysmal. He was confused, but I found it humorous: how did he succeed in half the test if he couldn't read? Instead of revealing aptitude, I think it was a stronger indication of his interests; he found the reading selections incredibly boring, so he skimmed and missed important details.

He found that his total score was only one point away from a larger scholarship in his first-choice college, however. He also learned that retaking the ACT raises the score for 60% of students, regardless of how much they study. So he had a statistical advantage for bettering his score with some serious work on his reading and English skills. He chose to play the odds and pay for another test.

It worked. He actually raised his score three points and obtained the scholarship he was looking for. And he did it all himself. I only worked with him on reading comprehension for about 30 minutes one afternoon.

7. Keep the scores in perspective.

Have I said this enough? Remind yourself and your student that this is just one test. He has many options once it's over, and how he handles his score reveals a lot about his self-awareness, humility, and perspective on life. Use this teaching moment wisely.

And also remember that this test does not predict future college success. Remember the high math scores and low reading comprehension on my son's test? His college experience has been the opposite! All of his general classes, including Bible, psychology, and English writing, were simple his first semester. The only class he's struggling in? Calculus, his favorite course. Go figure.

22. College and Beyond

Life isn't about finding yourself. Life is about creating
yourself.

-- George Bernard Shaw

WHEN WE LOOK back at our homeschool *why,* it's sobering to see how close we are to finishing our pursuit of it. Whatever our reasons for starting the homeschool journey, time is nearly up. In just a few short months, God will say, "Pencils down. Pass the papers in. The homeschool test is finished."

How will we do? Will God weigh us and find us wanting? Or will we hear, "Well done, thou good and faithful homeschool servant?" Sometimes it is hard to tell. Sometimes, we may wish for a do-over. But all the time, if we stay focused on our true homeschool priorities, this day of reckoning can be a joyous anticipation.

It's time to launch our young adults.

We are finished with the worst of it. Our student is making his life choices, living out his beliefs, finding his path, and becoming the person God created him to be. Maybe he will take a circuitous path. Probably he will make a lot of mistakes. Several times, he will scare us to death. Utimately it's time to let him go with God.

Did we do right? Have we prepared him adequately for the next year or two or ten of his life? Have we homeschooled responsibly? Have we made the grade, cut the mustard, and aced the test?

We will not find out for a long time. God is not through molding our young person, and He definitely is not through changing *us* every day to be more conformed to the image of Himself. In the meantime, while we wait and pray and counsel and pray some more, we can look back on some of the most important lessons we taught our teen (whether he was listening or not).

How to get a job and keep it.

One of the best things we have done for our teens is requiring them to work. I was not sure about that decision at first, but over time, it has proven to be the single best motivation for maturity in our young people. Ironically, the more hours they work, the higher their grades, too.

The first serious job my oldest landed was a part-time position with the dry cleaner down the street. He already had experience refereeing soccer games on weekends and evenings, but this was his first time working every day Monday through Friday. He was excited to work more hours. He interviewed for the job on his own, and he was proud of landing it.

Suddenly, the second or third week into the job, he quit talking about it. He would not tell me his next week's schedule. He would not tell me how his day was. He completely clammed up. Then one day, he said he had the next few days off, and that just felt . . . *off.*

This went on for a couple more days until he got a phone call and suddenly, he relaxed and told me he needed a ride back to work. That's when he told me the entire story.

His second week on the job, he had been fired. The owner told him that after he finished out that week, not to come back. He was devastated and embarrassed, so he wouldn't tell his parents he lost his job. He applied online for others while he kept going into work for the remaining days. He not only kept showing up, but he worked as hard as he could, doing extra tasks his boss hadn't assigned him and asking other employees how he could help.

This odd reaction to being fired made an impression on the owner. When my son was finally gone, the owners sorely missed his initiative. This is why he was rehired. After that, he was quickly trained to manage the facility in the owner's absence. Within a few months, he was hiring, training, and firing employees; translating and negotiating disputes between the workers and owners; and delivering the day's cash to the owner at the end of the week. His character and hard work earned him a reputation that far exceeded his chronological age.

Obviously, all of that happened on his own; he was not about to tell his parents what was going on until the dust was settled and he had solved his first serious employment problem. In the end, his tenacity and leadership revealed that at least two of our homeschool values (hard work and love for others) had taken root in his character.

How to manage his time and responsibilities.

Time management is the second life skill that concerned me when our son left home. Would he show up to classes on time? Would he remember his tests and assignments? Would he drop the ball and spend all day playing video games? I asked him repeatedly if I could buy him a planner or show him tricks on Google calendar. Again no, he wanted to try on his own.

The high school years, however, provide our teen with plenty of time to practice being responsible. By gradually handing over more and more control to our student, we give him valuable experience making wise choices with his time. So, yeah, maybe I do a lot of nagging freshman year. However, by sophomore year, the teen understands what needs to be done and how to do it. By junior year, there are very few reminders, merely accountability and grading.

My daughter is even more mature in this area than her older brother was. By age fifteen, she was completely independent in her school work; I just proctored tests and graded assignments. She managed her work schedule, put her own appointments on the family calendar, and arranged for her own transportation to events. Other than reminders to wash the dishes and pick up her bedroom (*cough, cough*), she needed little oversight. She already recognized that making wise choices in what she eats, how much sleep she gets, how hard she works, and how she manages her time with friends all contribute to how successful she is in achieving her goals – even if her goal is more time with her dog in front of the TV.

How to make friends and work with others.

Another issue our teen faces is socialization. These high school situations are just a sample of what our teen will face in college, the workplace, church, and adult life. Training our student to be loyal, kind, respectful, and loving is so much more than lecturing: it is humbly changing our own lives every day.

How to recognize and admit his errors.

One of the most important skills we can teach our student is *humility,* especially academic humility. This is something that bothered me about homeschool graduates for many years, to the point that I questioned if we should homeschool high school at all. The very last thing I wanted to produce was a snobby, prideful know-it-all who couldn't consider an opposing viewpoint if it came down from Mount Sinai.

There are many opportunities, however, to cultivate a teachable spirit in our young person. Giving him the grades he deserves (not the A's we want) helps. Challenging him with hard books, difficult issues, and the messy past is another. Encouraging him to say "I don't know" and "I could have done better" without

250

condemnation. Even openly admitting when we don't have answers, consistency, or virtue ourselves.

My college son is earned high marks in all of his classes . . . except for calculus. He struggled with that course from the beginning, and at times he wondered if he would even pass. Yet every time he talked about it, he insisted, "This is the class I don't understand, and I *love it!* I am going to learn things I've never imagined! That's why I'm here!"

It is, son. It's why we are all here: to see our needs, to learn and grow, and to glorify God while doing that.

How to write an essay and research paper.

The single greatest homeschool lesson my mother gave me was *how to write.* It is obviously what I do every day (though I never imagined it at the time). It is the skill I most used in college myself.

So writing is also the one study skill I am most careful to teach my own students. If a teen can write a complete sentence, put those sentences correctly into a paragraph, and then string his paragraphs into a logically constructed essay, he can communicate anything to anyone. Not only that, but his teachers will think he is brilliant.

Writing is the one skill my college student has most frequently thanked me for teaching him. "I'm getting better English grades than the English majors!" That is all I needed to hear.

23. The Secret

Command and teach these things. Let no one despise you for your youth, but set the believers an example in speech, in conduct, in love, in faith, in purity. Until I come, devote yourself to the public reading of Scripture, to exhortation, to teaching. Do not neglect the gift you have, which was given you by prophecy when the council of elders laid their hands on you. Practice these things, immerse yourself in them, so that all may see your progress. Keep a close watch on yourself and on the teaching. Persist in this, for by so doing you will save both yourself and your hearers.

-- 1 Timothy 4:11-16

MY PURPOSE in writing this book was not just to add yet another homeschool book on your shelf. I wanted more than just yet another guide to creating transcripts and planning high school courses.

Quite frankly, you can get all of that with a quick google search. Homeschoolers have been passing

ACTs and SATs for years, submitting transcripts to colleges for a couple generations, and successfully graduating into adulthood by the millions. Simply getting you over the finish line is not my goal.

Instead, I want to help you reframe your questions entirely. I want to shake up your view of homeschooling high school and cause you to question everything you are doing. It is my prayer you will be disturbed and frustrated until you search once more for the entire purpose of your homeschool.

Because that is exactly how God grows us and changes us. It is when our foundations are shaken, when the trials overwhelm us, when the tasks seem too hard and the foes too fierce that we finally look to Him. That is when we cry out to God for His plan, His provision, and His power.

No matter where you are in your homeschooling, no matter how long you've been at it or how much you think you know or how successful your plan has been up to this point, I'm praying that you will stop and ask yourself the big homeschool *why*. Seek God's purpose in your lesson plans right now. Make that front and center. Then watch everything else simply fall into place.

24. Take Action

Get started

☐ **Find your why.** Have you thought through and listed all the reasons you are homeschooling? Are you and your spouse on the same page in your homeschool efforts? Can you tell yourself, your student, your friends *why* you are homeschooling through the high school years? Take some time to list your reasons and share them with someone.

☐ **Connect with your purpose.** What is your role in homeschooling, mom? Are you taking on more than you should?

☐ **Get ready.** Is your teen prepared for high school work? Check the list in chapter 2, then make plans to shore up the skills he may be lacking.

☐ **Capture the big picture.** Are you clear what should be accomplished each year in high school? Do you know what you need to do this year, and what can wait for next year? Take a look at the year-by-year overview in chapter 3 to see where you are in your journey.

☐ **Know your unique style.** How clear are you on your student's learning style and how to maximize it? How confident are you about your own teaching style and how it works in high school? Take some time to study the overview in chapter 4 to find that happy sweet spot in your own unique homeschool style.

☐ **Envision a typical week.** Ok, stop laughing, we all know there's no typical week. But have you imagined how a calm, productive, manageable week would work for your teen? Have you worked with your teen to find how best to manage their time and responsibilities? Peek at my daughter's weekly routine in chapter 6, then outline your own.

Plan the courses

☐ **Research your state's graduation requirements.** Simply google "[your state] graduation requirements." Bookmark them, print them out, or copy them into your homeschool lesson planner.

☐ **Calculate the number of credits your student should take the first years of high school.** Use the handy math problem I gave you in chapter 12.

☐ **Sketch out your student's four years of courses.** Fill in the required courses first, starting from the freshman year with each one. Just write in general names, not exact curriculum: "English 1" not "American literature."

☐ **Pat yourself on the back.** Don't you feel better? Your student likely needs *less* than you were about to cram onto his plate. If your student has already completed courses, go ahead and write those in or cross them off. See how few are left? *You got this!*

☐ **Let your student chose any remaining courses.** Do you have one credit of science left with no specific requirement? Hand your student a homeschool catalog or two and let him choose! Are you left with a couple empty credits in the senior year? Ask your student what *he* wants to do with them!

Parent sensitively

- ☐ **Is your teen gravitating toward a different parent?** Plan with your spouse ways to accommodate him.

- ☐ **Is your teen quiet, distant, too busy to talk, or moody?** Find what environment or situations make it easier for him to talk, and make it as easy to come to you as possible.

- ☐ **Does your teen have more emotional outbursts or arguments?** Recognize he has growing pressures and frustrations on top of confusing hormonal changes. Try to recall how difficult everything seemed when *you* were his age.

- ☐ **Do you struggle with discipline?** Try to focus on *natural consequences* of behavior instead of arbitrary punishments. Give one or two warnings (if he is 10 minutes late from curfew, remind him he could lose his keys). Then follow through. Teens learn from their mistakes more than from our words, so these difficult times are crucial parenting moments.

Encourage friendships

- ☐ **Does your teen nurture relationships from a variety of age groups and backgrounds?** Help him recognize the important people around him, not just his own age group.

- ☐ **Does your teen complain of loneliness?** Listen carefully and ask him what he is specifically looking for.

- ☐ **Is your teen involved in a variety of social opportunities?** Help him find church ministries, community volunteer organizations, and other service groups to work in. Make sure he has a job that keeps him busy. Even look at sports, music, or drama classes. In every situation, gently encourage him to find *someone* who needs a friend or helper. By investing himself in others, he will find the relationships he craves.

☐ **Are you hovering?** Now is the time to step back and let the teen take charge of his relationships. Do not micromanage his communication, ministry, or even classes. Let him make some mistakes and learn from them.

Consider dating

☐ **Have you talked frequently about marriage and family issues?** Now is when we *hope* that our values are already obvious to our teens, but maybe we missed something. Take advantage of casual conversation and off-hand opportunities to say a few brief words about the sanctity of marriage and the importance of fidelity.

☐ **Does your teen know the difference between biblical principles and opinions?** As strongly as we feel about these issues, it is vitally important our teens know what *God* says about the subject. Take time to share these truths with your young person.

☐ **Do you make a distinction between choice and rules?** Make sure you and your spouse are on the same page about dating rules for your family and be clear what is *your house rules,* what is *biblical truth,* and what is *opinion and advice.* Being clear about these distinctions helps the relationship overall; teens appreciate our honesty. There are times we come down hard and say, "Thus saith the Lord." And there are many times we assert our great advice. Yet sometimes we just have to say, "Sorry if you don't agree, but as long as you're under 18 (or living at home, or dependent on us, whatever the limit is in your house), this is the rule. When you are out on your own, you make your own rules."

☐ **Does your teen ask you health, sexuality, and dating questions?** If not, find out where he *is* getting his information. On more than one occasion, my husband has reminded our sons that their friends do *not* have first-hand information on these subjects. It may be fun to

265

joke with the guys, but when it comes down to it, only dad knows reality. So consider the source and sensitively offer more accurate and comprehensive information.

Support work and ministry

☐ **Does your teen have financial responsibilities?** Be sure to set up the *need* to work first by letting him *want* for some things: luxuries, extra clothes, electronics, phone, car, etc.

☐ **Are you allowing your teen to find his own job?** Give a few ideas, tell him some tips for his first interview, but let him struggle through this himself. Finding a job and convincing a business owner to hire him are important skills he needs to learn on his own.

☐ **Have you set some work expectations?** Look through my sample guidelines in chapter 16 and find what house rules work best for your teen.

☐ **Is your teen involved in the church and community?** Require volunteer service every semester, and be sure you are setting the example personally. Serving together as a family is ideal.

Brave teen driving

☐ **Do you know the teen driving laws in your state?** Check your state's department of motor vehicles online website.

☐ **Have you set the teen driving rules for your family?** Talk through the issues with your spouse, especially in these areas:

   o   What vehicles can your teen drive?

   o   Who is responsible for gas, maintenance, license fees, and insurance?

   o   Who is your teen allowed to drive with?

   o   What happens if your teen gets a ticket? An auto accident?

☐ **Are you comfortable allowing your teen to drive away?** Examine the character of your teen, and pray the Lord will allow that to continue to develop into maturity.

- ☐ **Does your teen still recognize your authority?** Be consistent in your parenting to provide the stability and protection he needs.

Prepare for graduation

Academically

- ☐ **Has your student completed the requirements for high school graduation in your state?** Search for your state's guidelines online.
- ☐ **Has your student completed the requirements for admission to the college of his choice?** Contact the admissions office for a list of what courses they expect to see on a transcript.
- ☐ **Have you created a high school transcript for your student?** Again, contact your college admissions office for a sample transcript, and be sure to grab my free transcript builder at lagarfias.com/transcripts.

☐ **Has your student narrowed down his choice of colleges?** Encourage him to take the lead on communications with admissions offices and faculty; it makes a good impression and empowers him to make the decision.

☐ **Has your student sent his test results to the maximum number of colleges?** Even if he knows what school he wants to go to, encourage him to send the results to several schools. You never know what they may offer when they see those scores.

Financially

☐ **Does your teen have a regular job?** If not, push him out the door to get one for himself. Make him pay something (anything!) as an incentive, and encourage him to save for college expenses, too.

☐ **Does your teen know how to manage his finances?** As soon as he gets his first paycheck, help him open an account. Teach him how to reconcile his statements, use his debit card wisely, and save responsibly.

☐ **Does your teen know how to pay bills?** Make him responsible for his gas, his mobile phone, his entertainment, and other expenses. Help him anticipate his monthly expenditures so he can begin budgeting wisely. These are important lessons teens cannot understand without experience, and the skills help guard against one of the biggest pitfalls in college: debt.

Relationally

☐ **Does your teen respect adults around him and seek advice from his parents, teachers, pastor, and others?** This is a good indication of a teachable spirit.

☐ **Does your teen live consistently with his own beliefs?** Even if he doesn't share your convictions in everything, he should begin deciding what kind of adult he wants to be and living in accordance to his own standards.

- ☐ **Does your teen demonstrate love and compassion to others?** This is the second most important commandment, yet entirely contrary to the egocentric life stage that he is growing into.

- ☐ **Does your teen wrestle with his faith?** This is when he decides *for himself* if he will attend church, if he will be a true Christian, if he will seek godly friends, if he will live for the Lord. He will question the rules and standards he was brought up with, weigh them against what he knows to be true, and determine what he will keep and what he will discard. This is *very healthy*. The best way to support his faith journey is to calmly answer his questions and point him to more resources for information and people for advice, all while affirming your own love and commitment to him.

Lovingly

- ☐ **Does your teen know when you consider him an adult?** Much of my twenties, I spent

271

struggling to validate myself, to somehow prove I was an adult. I've seen other twenty-somethings wrestle with the same frustration, craving respect as an adult. I want my young adult to know when he is in the driver's seat, at what point he's taking control of his life decisions. I had a talk in the backyard one sunny afternoon with my firstborn, during which I used the solemn words, "I now look at you as an adult. You make the choices that are right for your life, and I will always be here to support you and love you." (There may have been tears. I cried a little, too.) His father took him on a special "man trip" vacation for the two of them, during which they talked about serious grown-up things and he was formally recognized by his father as a man. These rites of passage are sacred moments to growing adults, and our other children and teens are eagerly looking forward to their own adulthood ceremonies.

☐ **Have you set the house rules for adult children?** Talk through the issues with your spouse, then communicate them clearly to your new adult, especially in these areas:

o   Is there a curfew?

o   If the young adult is living at home, are there financial contributions expected?

o   What are the financial agreements between student and parent for college?

o   What happens if the student leaves college or fails to launch? Can he come home? Under what conditions?

o   What are the dating rules for adult children at home?

o   How should the young adult show proper respect for the house rules younger siblings still live under (like curfew, dating, entertainment, etc)?

☐   **How should the parents and adult children demonstrate mutual respect, love, and consideration?** This is an ongoing talk in our home as we feel through this issue together. So far maintaining an open dialog, being sensitive when he asks for more personal space (or less nagging), and clearly stating expectations has gone a long way toward minimizing difficulties.

Tips from Friends

Remember that advanced placement doesn't necessarily have to mean early high school graduation. Even if your students are ready academically, they might find it socially and emotionally tough to transition to the rigors of full-time college life (even junior college) one or two years before their traditionally schooled friends. Be sure they have reached appropriate emotional maturity before launching them into the world.

Traci Matt, author of *Don't Waste Don't Waste Your Time Homeschooling*

I keep homeschooling easy by giving my daughters (ages 11, 9, and 7) the opportunity to be as independent as possible as young as possible in their learning process. They take my weekly outline for our lessons and use it themselves to do what they can on their own, they check in with me when they are done, and then we work together on what we need to.

275

Melissa Williamson of

gracefilledhomeschooling.blogspot.com

Keep homeschool easy. You don't have to check off all the boxes in your teacher's guides! Make your curriculum work for you instead of letting it dictate everything you do, and take charge of it. Skip what doesn't work or fit, and move at your own pace.

Anne Campbell of mylearningtable.com

To keep our homeschool easy I have to remember to do two things: have a plan and be flexible. Both are essential and keep my perspective in just the right place.

Kim Brush of daytodayadventures.com

My son really wanted to get a head start on college ASAP. So, once he started high school, for every summer he worked ahead two subjects as his summer school. Since I usually have small assignments to do during the summer anyway, it wasn't anything new to him. By the time his junior year came around -

he had finished all his requirements for high school! His senior year he was able to enroll in college courses.

Becky Corbin - Homeschooler of five children for over thirteen years.

I don't always have time to write down all the books read during the year that we get from the library. It's easier to stack them up and take a picture with my smart phone! When I find a few minutes throughout the year, I'll add them to the spreadsheet.

Jackie Ryan Masek of LJSkool.com

My quickest and easiest tips: If it feels like everyone needs a break, take a break. Leave some space in your plans for catch-up time. Don't be afraid to change. When something isn't working, take a step back and figure out what will work for you and your family.

Ashley Fox of somerandomlady.com

Do all the planning and scheduling you want, comparing state graduation requirements and college entrance requirements. But realize that these are the final years of intensive discipleship that God has given us. Focus on the relationship and building memories. Those will do more to help your child remain in the faith than the academics in the college and beyond years. What does it profit a mom to perfectly execute the curriculum and yet lose the souls of her students to the world?

Anni Welborne

Made in the USA
Middletown, DE
21 January 2021